SWARAJ

SWARAJ:
CULTURAL AND POLITICAL

PRAMATHA NATH BOSE

GYAN

Published by

Gyan Publishing House
5, Ansari Road
Daryaganj, New Delhi-110002
Phone: 011-47034999, 9811692060
E-mail: books@gyanbooks.com

Distribution Network
gyanbooks.com
India, USA, Canada, UK, Australia

ISBN: 978-93-7014-088-2 (PB)

First Published, 1929

2nd Impression 2025

Printed at: Gyan Press, Delhi.

SWARAJ

Author: PRAMATHA NATH BOSE

Swaraj—Cultural and Political

BY

PRAMATHA NATH BOSE, B. SC. LOND.

AUTHOR OF A "HISTORY OF HINDU CIVILIZATION UNDER BRITISH RULE", "EPOCHS OF CIVILIZATION" &C.

"Do not accept anything that is either written or spoken by any teacher of any epoch or age unless such harmonises with reason and bears the test of examination."

Gautama Buddha.

W. NEWMAN & CO., LTD.

3, OLD COURT HOUSE STREET, CALCUTTA.

1929

CONTENTS.

Erratum—p. 26, line 7, omit (now Lord Meston)

Swaraj—Cultural and Political

CHAPTER I.

INDIA HITHERTO A NATION.

I

There is no statement more common in the West and in new India than that India has hitherto not been a nation, but a mere heterogeneous congeries of races, sects and creeds ; and that she is just now in the birth-throes of nationhood under Western influence. To our mind, the reverse of this statement is true. India has hitherto been a nation which is now being disintegrated.*

---

* "It is sometimes said by friends of India," observes Dr. Anand K. Coomarswamy, "that the National movement is the natural result of English education, and one, of which England should in truth be proud, as showing that under 'civilization' and Pax Britannica, Indians are becoming at last capable of self-government. The facts are otherwise. If Indians are still capable of self-government, it is in spite of all the anti-national tendencies of a system of education that has ignored or despised almost every ideal informing the national culture."

"Essays in National Idealism," p. 96

There are three fundamental unities which in varying degrees of preponderance underlie the conception of nationhood *viz.*, geographical, cultural, and political.

Geographical Unity.

Sanskrit literature abundantly testifies to the gradual evolution of the notion of the geographical unity of India. During the earlier period of their settlement the Indo-Aryans considered Northern India, which they called Aryavarta, to be their home. The rivers invoked by the Aryan Rishis in their prayers were confined to Aryavarta—the Ganga, the Jamuna, the Sarasvati, the Satadru (Sutlej), the Parusni (Ravi), the Asikni (Chenab), the Vitasta (Jhelum), the Arjikiya (Beas), and the Susoma (Indus). As they spread over Southern India, their geographical outlook was widened, and they came to regard India, as we know it now, to be their country. The rivers of the South then claimed an equal share of their veneration as is evidenced by the following hymn which replaced the narrower one of the Rigveda :

Gange cha Yamune chaiba
Godavari Sarasvati,
Narmade Sindhu-Kaveri Jalesmin
Sannidhim kuru.

[O Ganga, Yamuna, Godavari, Sarasvati, Narmada, Indus and Kaveri, approach this water offered by me.]

The catalogue of sacred places which are resorted to by all Hindu pilgrims was expanded so as to embrace those of the south such as Kanchi (Conjeveram) and Ramesvara and that of sacred mountains was enlarged so as to comprise Mahendra (the Eastern Ghats) and Malaya and Sahya (the Western Ghats). Reformers like Samkaracharya and Chaitanya made a tour of the whole of India, and the former emphasized his idea of its unity by establishing *Maths* in the north (the Himalaya, Jyotirmath), the south (Sringeri), the East (Gobardhan at Puri) and the West (Sarada at Dwaraka).

II

Cultural Unity in pre-Mahomedan times.

As the Aryans spread from the banks of the Indus, they came in collision with the aborigines, who, naturally enough, opposed their advance, fought them, disturbed their sacrifice, and harassed them in endless ways. For such acts, which no doubt appeared to the Aryans as acts of doubtful courtesy, they called their adversaries, "Dasyus" ("robbers"); "Rakshas" ("evil spirits,") &c. Epithets of the grossest invective were heaped on the devoted heads of the poor aborigines. They are described as irreligious, impious, and lowest of the low; they are also in some texts contemptuously called *black-skinned*—a very significant epithet, as the Sanskrit term for 'Caste' primarily means colour, which according to some scholars points to an original difference of colour as the first origin of caste. The Aryan immigrants, like the dominant races of ancient Peru and Egypt, had a fairer colour than the aborigines. Thus, during the Rigvedic period, there were, if I may so express myself, two 'colors'—the fair (Aryan), and the black (Dasyuite or Dása). But the Aryans ultimately succeeded in conquering and subjugating their opponents ; and instead of exterminating the conquered tribes, or reducing them to a condition of slavery, they followed a policy characterised by mercy and humanity. The aboriginal tribes—now called Sudras—were incorporated with the Aryan society though on the hard condition, that they should occupy the lowest position in it.

As they spread among the aborigines whether as conquerors or as colonists, the Aryans propagated their culture among them. The Aryanisation of the aborigines, gradually reacted upon the original religious system of the Aryas. It is probable that the different forms of demonolatry prevalent among the various sections of the aborigines, especially the Dravidians of the South, shaped, moulded and refined by Aryan thought, gave rise to Saivism. We do not know the exact steps which led to the transformation of the Vedic Rudra into the Mahadeva of later Hinduism. It was however an accomplished fact in the earlier centuries of the Christian era. The Indian Dionysos of Megasthenes is usually indentified with Siva. Sivaite figures alternating with Buddhist symbols are represented on coins of the Indo-Scythian kings, about the beginning of the Christian era. Siva is the great patron of the ancient dramatic and other literatures. He is represented in a twofold character—the terror-inspiring and the beneficent. He is the Auspicious, as well as the Terrible. His wife also appears in similar double character. She is Uma, the gracious, and Ambika, the good mother, as well as Kali, the black one, and Karala, the horrible. In these two-fold aspects we trace, however indistinctly, the fusion of Aryan and non-Aryan conceptions of the Divinity, the former beneficent and lovable, the latter destructive and terrible.

Thus there arose that grand synthesis of religions which is known in history as Hinduism, and which embraces all shades of religious thought from the Vedantism of the highly cultured Aryan to the fetishism and animism of the aborigines. Though professedly based upon the Vedas, it is no more like the

Vedic religion than man is like the protoplasmic germ out of which he is supposed to have been evolved. It is not the creed of the Rigveda, nor of the Brahmanas, nor of the Upanishads, nor of the Puranas ; it is neither Saivism, nor Vaishnavism, nor Saktism ; yet it is all these. The key note of Hinduism is struck by Srikrishna in the Bhagavatgita:

"However men approach Me, even so do I welcome them, for the path men take from every side is Mine."

There is a remarkable unity in the diversity of the forms of faith comprised under Hinduism. Though there are numerous Saiva, Vaishnava and other sects, the number of sectaries is comparatively insignificant. The majority of the Hindu community accept the whole system of Hindu mythology. Preference for any particular deity does not preclude the worship of the other deities. Sectarianism, that is strict adhesion to one divinity or one faith is quite unusual. The same Hindu will often in one round of pilgrimage visit temples dedicated to Siva, Krishna, the Devi, Rama, Ganesh or Hanuman. The same Hindu will often in the course of one year celebrate the worship of these and various other divinities ; and if he is philosophically disposed, he will with Bhartrihari exclaim: "One god, Siva or Krishna."

The ethical principles which underlie the various subdivisions of Hinduism including Buddhism and Jainism, are altruism, renunciation and *Karma*.

It is their ethical development which enabled the Hindus to integrate the foreign elements into their system of civilization, and thus place it on a stable basis. It is with ethical development that the racial cleavage between the Aryans and the non-Aryans began to disappear, and they were gradually fused into one nation, known in history as the Hindu, inspired by the same ideals and worshipping the same gods and goddesses. India suffered repeated invasions from outside, by the Greeks, the Parthians, the Scythians and the Huns, who succeeded in establishing their authority in various parts of the country. Sooner or later, however, they were either expelled or became Hinduised, adopting the Hindu religion, the Hindu literature and the Hindu institutions. The Greek Menander who had his capital at Kabul (about the middle of the second century B.C.) became a convert to Buddhism—an offshoot of Hinduism—and has been immortalised under the name of Milinda in the celebrated Buddhist work entitled "The Questions of Milinda." The Scythian (Kushan) Kadphisis II was an ardent votary of Siva, and his successors, Kanishka and his son Hushka, were enthusiastic followers of Buddhism. The

Pallavas of Parthian origin, who for four centuries were the premier power in southern India, were completely Hinduised, and Kanchi (Conjeveram) has since their time been one of the most important strongholds of Hinduism. The Saka (Scythian) Satraps of Surastra (Kathiawar) adopted either the Brahmanical or the Buddhist cult of Hinduism.

The Hindus like the Chinese have never, since they attained the highest stage of their civilization some centuries before the Christian era, been pervaded by the military and the predatory spirit. Altruism has always been with them the most important of the cardinal virtues. As in China, so in India, wealth never formed the basis of social rank; wisdom and virtue were held in the highest esteem, and there was perfect freedom of thought.

Cultural Unity in Mahomedan times.

The incursions and invasions of the Mahomedans for a time exerted a disintegrating influence upon Indian nationhood. But Hindu culture ultimately succeeded not only in opposing it but also in capturing the Moslem mind and strongly influencing Moslem culture and Moslem administration. Settled in India the Mahomedans by degrees became more or less Hinduised. The zeal for the propagation of Islam abated. The blind bigotry of the Moslem was gradually tempered by the philosophic culture of the Hindu, and Hindu influence on the religion and government of the Moslem gradually became more and more marked.

On the other hand, the uncompromising Monotheism of the Mahomedans exerted a strong and wholesome influence on Hinduism. It was chiefly this influence that produced that galaxy of earnest reformers who shed such lustre on India for three centuries from the fourteenth to the seventeenth. They all preached the unity of the Godhead; they all abjured caste-distinctions; and they all admitted Mahomedans into their sects. Ramananda, Kabir, Nanak and Chaitanya were four of the foremost among them. The catholicity of Kabir was so great, that to this day Mahomedans claim him as one of their persuasion. The thesis of one of Nanak's earliest sermons was—"There are neither Hindus nor Mahomedans."

The result of this wholesome action and reaction between Hinduism and Mahomedanism was a spirit of sympathy and amity which was accentuated by the fact, that while among the cultured classes Pantheism presented a point of contact between the two communities (the Sufism of the one being but little distinguishable from the Vedantism of the other), there were among the mass of the Mahomedans large numbers of converted Hindus who could not divest themselves of their prepossessions for the practices and prejudices of the religion they had abandoned, and shared the joys of Hindu processions and festivals.

The Hindus also joined the Mahomedans in such festivals as the Moharram. There were two principles common to Hindu and Mahomedan cultures which facilitated their assimilation and which were eminently favourable to peace and concord. One of these was Renunciation. The Hindus and Mahomedans vied with one another in paying homage to ascetic saints irrespective of their caste or creed. The Hindu Sadhus and Mahomedan Fakirs served as common bonds of the two communities.* Renunciation also made for amity in another way. It made the people generally lead a simple life and thus, on the one hand, avoid that intensity of the struggle for animal existence which is a fruitful source of jealousy and discord between individuals and classes, and on the other, devote their savings to charity and social service which cemented the different communities. Then, there was the principle of *Karma* among the Hindus and

* The bigoted Mahomedan historian, Khafi Khan, was horrified at the conduct of the Europeans of his day who did not allow "religious medicants to come into their bounds. When one found his way unawares, if he were a Hindu, he was subjected to such tortures as made his escape with life very doubtful, and if he were a Musalman he was imprisoned and worried for some days, and then set at liberty."

that of Fate among the Mahomedans. However they might differ in theory, in practice they made for contentment, and therefore, for peace and social harmony. The rural life which the people led almost universally, and substantial village self-government which they enjoyed and which made them to a great extent independent of the central Government were also important factors of unity between the various communities.

This amicable spirit was generally reflected in the policy of Governments, whether Hindu or Mahomedan. Knowing how strong Hindu feeling was about cow-killing, some of the emperors at Delhi endeavoured to check or stop it. In this connection the following advice given by Babar to his son Humayun is of considerable interest:

"O my son ! People of diverse religions inhabit India ; and it is a matter of thanksgiving to God, that the King of Kings has entrusted the government of this country to you. It therefore behoves you that—

1. You should not allow religious prejudices to influence your mind, and administer impartial justice having due regard to the religious susceptibilities and religious customs of all sections of the people.

2. In particular refrain from the slaughter of cows, which will help you to obtain a hold on the hearts of the people of India. Thus you

will bind the people of this land to yourself by ties of gratitude.

3. You should never destroy the places of worship of any community and always be justice-loving, so that the relations between the king and his subjects may remain cordial and there be peace and contentment in the land.

4. The propagation of Islam will be better carried on with the sword of love and obligation than with the sword of oppression.

5. Always ignore the mutual dissensions of Shias and Sunnis, otherwise they will lead to the weakness of Islam.

6. Treat the different peculiarities of your subjects as the different seasons of the year so that the body politic may remain free from disease."*

* Many anecdotes are told of the influence of Guru Nanak on Babar. When Babar destroyed the town of Eminabad and the neighbouring villages, there was a general massacre of the people, and Pathan as well as Hindu habitations were plundered and levelled to the ground. It is said that the Guru not approving this sort of Zulum managed to secure an interview with Babar, who, hearing of his pious movements in prison had rather himself desired to see him. The Guru's words had such a magic effect on his mind that he showed him a special respect while all his courtiers saluted him. The emperor asked him to accept a present from him. The Guru replied that he wanted nothing for himself, but requested that the captives of Eminabad might he released. Upon this the Emperor ordered that they should be set free and their properties, restored to them.

The brightest period of the Mahomedan Empire was unquestionably the period between the accession of Akbar and the deposition of Shahjahan, and it was during this period that Hindu-Moslem amity was best exhibited. Akbar prohibited the killing of cows, and performed the *Hom* (a Hindu ceremony). "He also introduced" says the orthodox Badaoni, "though modified by his peculiar views, Hindu customs and heresies into the court assemblies, and introduces them still in order to please and gain the good-will of the Hindus." Abul Fazal, his most cultured Mahomedan courtier, was

---

His Majesty was so pleased with the Guru that he asked him to accompany him. The Guru at first promised to remain only one day with him, but on being pressed to remain three days he at last consented. Once he was so affected that he fell into a trance and became unconscious. Babar was alarmed, and when the Guru stood up he prayed him to be gracious to him. The Guru replied, "If thou, O Emperor, desirest kindness, set all thy captives free." Babar agreed and the Guru said, "Thy empire shall remain for a long time." His Majesty on this ordered that all his prisoners should be clothed with robes of honour, a matter which caused the Guru much pleasure and satisfaction. Then the Emperor asked for instructions, and the Guru said, "Deliver just judgments, reverence holy men, forswear wine and gambling. The monarch who indulgeth in these vices shall, if he survives, bewail his misdeeds. Be merciful to the vanquished, and worship God in spirit and in truth."

—"Ramanand to Ram Tirath." pp. 46—47

held by some of his contemporaries to be a Hindu. Jehangir was the son of a Hindu wife of Akbar. Shah Jehan also was the offspring of a Hindu Queen of Jehangir. The pro-Hindu policy of Akbar was continued by both Jehangir and Shah Jehan. The contest between Dara and Aurangzeb was really a contest between enlightenment and bigotry. Dara wrote a book attempting to reconcile the Hindu and Mahomedan doctrines. He had translations made of fifty *Upanishads*. Aurangzeb triumphed. But his triumph was only temporary, ending with his reign and did not lead to any serious attenuation of Hindu-Moslem cordiality which lasted till about two generations ago. Speaking of the relation between Hindus and Mahomedans in the Deccan, Hamilton observes in his "East India Gazetteer (Published 1828) : "There is a considerable Mahomedan population in the countries subject to the Nizam, but those of the lower classes, who are cultivators, have nearly all adopted the manners and customs of the Hindus." In Rangpur district (Bengal) he noticed, "that the two religions are on the most friendly terms, and mutually apply to the deities and saints of the other, when they imagine that application to their own will be ineffectual." Speaking generally of Hindusthan he observes: "For almost a century past, the Mahomedans have evinced much deference to the prejudices of their Hindu neighbours, and strong prediliction towards many of their ceremonies." Dr. Taylor writing in 1839 says in his Topography of Dacca: "Religious quarrels between Hindus and Mahomedans are rare occurrences. These two classes live in perfect peace and concord, and a majority of the individuals belonging to them have even overcome their prejudices so far as to smoke from the same *hookah.*" Lord Meston, when Lieut. Governor of the United Provinces, observed:

"From time immemorial Hindus and Mahomedans have lived together at Ajodhya and Fyzabad in peace and amity. As a symbol of this happy unity you see Mahomedans worshipping at Babar's mosque and Hindus paying adoration at the shrine of Ramchandra's birth place within a few yards of each other, and within the same enclosure wall."

Political Unity the result of Cultural Unity.

Considerable political unity was the result of this friendly feeling. It was evidenced on one memorable occasion during British Rule. Canning who was Governor General at the time soon ceased to speak of the Sepoy War as a "mutiny," but called it a "rebellion" a "revolt." During the Mahomedan period Akbar realised the idea of the political unity of India as fully as Asoka did in Buddhist and Vikramditya in Hindu times. Emperors like Nasiruddin and Akbar could not have carried out their strongly pro-Hindu policy had there been any strong opposition from the Moslems. It was no doubt resented by some bigoted Moslems. Badaoni, for instance, writing about Akbar's reign makes this caustic observation : "The Hindus are of course indispensable ; to them belongs half the land and half the army. Neither the Hindusthanis (Musalmans settled in India), nor the Moguls can point to such grand lords as the Hindus have among themselves." But the fact, that men like Badaoni had to rest contented with such atrabiliar outbursts, shows that they had no backing among the people. On the other hand, the intolerant Anti-Hindn policy of the bigoted Aurangzeb met with vigorous opposition from the Hindus which ultimately led to the downfall of the Mogul Empire ; and it would seem that they were helped even by Government officials in this opposition. "The infidel inhabitants of the city and the country around," says Khafi Khan, "made great opposition to the payment of the Jezia (a capitation tax). There was not a district where the people with the help of the Faujdars did not make disturbances and resistance." Sirajadowla is another instance of a despot, though of a different type, to depose whom Hindus and Mahomedans joined hands.

Political unity under Moslem rule is also inferable from the fact, that Mahomedan sovereigns could ignore the communal principle in their administration without giving rise to serious discontent. They might have parasitic noodles hanging about their courts, but they generally selected for responsible posts the best men available regardless of caste or creed. Not to speak of Akbar, whose most trusted councillors were the Hindus, Mansing, Todar Mull and Birbal and the Hinduised Mahomedans, Abul Fazal and Faizi, the fittest men were generally appointed irrespective of their caste or creed even by Mahomedan rulers without pro-Hindu proclivities, at least of a pronounced character. *

* During the reigns of the Emperors Feroksir, Rafi-ud-Darjat, Rafi-u-dowla and part of the reign of Mohomed Shah Ratan Chand, who was Deputy Vizier, enjoyed immense influence. Ibrahim, king of Golconda, had Jagdeo for his prime minister. When Alivardi Khan became Governor of Bengal he appointed as his prime minister Janakiram. Mohanlal was the trusted minister of Sirajadowla. Among his other officers who held high positions of trust were Durlavram and Ram Narayan.

CHAPTER II.

INDIA'S CULTURAL SWARAJ.

India's cultural empire.

From what has been said in the last chapter, it will be seen, that the cultural bond of Indian nationhood was much stronger than the political. And when Westerners and Westernised Indians talk of calling forth Indian nationhood they have this fact in view, because they attach inordinate importance to politics and consider the political to be the main, if not the sole, bond of nationhood. The Swaraj which India enjoyed was primarily cultural. As we shall see hereafter, with real village self-government, the people were more or less independent of the central government. Ever since India attained the ethical, the highest stage of civilization,* her empire extended nearly all over Asia, but it was the empire of culture with peace and altruism as its basic principles, won and maintained not by physical but by psychic force. The cultural contrast between India and the West was pointed out to Alexander the Great by the ascetic Dandin:

"We honour God, love man, neglect gold and contemn death ; you, on the other hand,

---

* The writer has dealt with the various stages of Civilization in his "Epochs of Civilization,"

fear death, honour gold, hate man, and contemn God. Your mind is filled with vast desires and insatiable avarice and a diabolical thirst for Empire. You are made much like other men, and yet you would obtain by force whatever mankind possesses."

The Indo-Aryans have conferred enormous benefits upon large masses of people in India and outside India, in Tibet, Ceylon, Burma, China, Indo-China, Japan and Malay Archipelago and Central America, not by conquering or annexing their territories or exploiting them materially, but by settling among them and exerting the irresistable influence of intellectual and spiritual superiority. The system of Laotsze, the greatest philosopher China has produced, corresponds so closely to Vedantism, that he is supposed by some to have drawn his inspiration from India, unless, indeed, as some suppose, he was an Indian by birth. "Siam received", says Mr. Cobaton, "its first civilization from the Brahmins of India, and then from the merchants from the Malabar and the Coromondal coast......There are still extant noteworthy archæological witnesses of this primitive Hinduisation of Siam in the monuments of its former capitals. ......The former and present religions of Siam (Brahmanism and Buddhism), its sacred language, its civil institutions, its writing, its arts and its literature came from India." "The oldest foreign loan words in Malay are Sanskrit, including words for religious, moral and intellectual ideas, with some astronomical, mathematical and botanical terms, a court vocabulary and a large number of everyday words. In their pantheon the greater gods are Hindu while the lesser gods are Malay. Their cosmology is also Hindu."*

The Mexican idea of the four ages or Yugas resembles that of the Buddhists, as does also that of the nine stages of heaven and hell. The Toltec tradition of the mysterious Quetzalcoatl, who is described as a fair man with "noble features, long black hair, and full beard, dressed in flowing robes" and as a "saintly ruler," probably refers to a Buddhist missionary. He is said to have dwelt twenty years among the Toltecs (one of the most ancient of the civilized races of Central America), and taught them to "follow his austere and ascetic life, to hate all violence and war, to sacrifice no men or beasts on the altars, but to give mild offerings of bread and flowers and perfumes." Such a mild doctrine could not in the earlier centuries of the Christian era have come from any other quarter than Eastern Asia. Legend tells stories of the mysterious visitor teaching the Toltecs "picture-writing and the calendar,

* Dr. Kalidas Nag, "Greater India Society Bulletin No. 1."

and also the artistic work of the silversmith for which Cholula was long famed."

In the West, the Buddhist missionaries of Asok carried the message of peace and universal amity to Syria, Egypt, Macedonia and Epirus ; and there are erudite scholars who have traced the influence of Buddhism on the early development of Christianity.

The Medical science of the West was strongly influenced by that of the Hindus. Numerous drugs of Indian origin are noticed by the Greeks. It is even supposed by some that Hippocrates borrowed from the Hindus. Charaka, the oldest Hindu writer on medical subjects whose works have come down to us, is referred to by Serapion, one of the earliest of the Arab physicians, as well as by Avicenna and Rahzes. A variety of treatises on medical science were translated from the Sanskrit into Arabic and Persian, and two Hindu physicians Mankeh and Saleh, the former of whom translated a special Sanskrit treatise on poison into Persian, held appointments as body physicians to Harun-ul-Rashid. The Saracens introduced the Indian method of Arithmetic and the Indian Algebra and Chemistry into Europe.

From a very remote period, India has been divided into a number of small principalities. Megasthenes counted 118 and Hiouen Thsang 76. The Kings who were most powerful exacted submission from weaker princes, but such submission was in the majority of cases merely nominal. Even in the case of conquest, it is enjoined in the Manusamhita, that "immediate security is to be assured to all by proclamation. The religion and laws of the country are to be respected and as soon as time has been allowed for ascertaining that the conquered people are to be trusted, a prince of the royal family of the conquered country is to be placed on the throne who should hold his kingdom as a dependency." That this law was not a mere camouflage is proved by the fact that the majority of the Kings of India have been either Hinduised aborigines or low caste Hindus. The Brahmans, the highest caste, never, as a class, sought material aggrandisement. Government, trade, in short every occupation calculated to further material interests they left to the lower classes. What they sought to restrict within the two highest classes, and especially within their own class, was spiritual and intellectual advancement which is of much more abiding value to a nation and to humanity than material aggrandisement. And under their wise guidance India maintained cultural Swaraj which made her prosperous despite numerous political revolutions.

Ethical and spiritual culture

As the writer has shown in his "National Education and Modern Progress," the primary object of high education in India was ethical and spiritual culture. It was carried down to the mass of the people by vernacular translations of works like the Ramayana and the Mahabharata, popular dramatic entertainments, etc. That ethical culture in Ancient India was not confined to literature and inscriptions but was to a large extent realised by the people in their lives is testified to by intelligent foreigners (Greeks and Chinese) who sojourned in India long enough to be able to form a correct estimate of its condition.* Coming to more recent times, Idrisi in his Geography (written in the 11th century A. D.) says : "The Indians are naturally inclined to justice and never depart from it in their action. Their good faith, honesty and fidelity to their engagements are wellknown, and they are so famous for these qualities that people flock to their country from every side." Marco Polo (13th century) observed, "you must know that these Brahmins are the best merchants in the world and the most truthful, they would not tell a lie for anything on earth." Abul Fazl, the accomplished author of the *Ain-i-Akbari* (16th century) notes : "The Hindus are admirers of truth and unbounded fidelity in all dealings."

During the earlier part of the British Rule, Col. Sleeman assures us that "falsehood or lying between members of the

* "Vide "Epochs of Civilization" pp. 187—191.

same village is almost unknown" He adds, "I have had before me hundreds of cases in which a man's property, liberty and life have depended upon his telling a lie, and he has refused to tell it."

Warren Hastings spoke of the modern Hindus as "gentle, benevolent, more susceptible of gratitude for kindness shown them than prompted to vengeance for wrongs inflicted, and as exempt from the worst propensities of human passion as any people upon the face of the earth ; they are faithful, and affectionate in service and submissive to legal authority ......The precepts of their religion are wonderfully fitted to promote the best ends of society, its peace and good order."

Bishop Heber spoke of them as "decidedly by nature, a mild, pleasing, and intelligent race ; sober, parsimonious and, when an object is held out to them, most industrious and persevering," and as "constitutionally kind-hearted, industrious, sober, and peaceable."

Abbe Du Bois speaking of the Hindus says : "They will never suffer the needy who have implored their charity to go unassisted ....What the European possesses, he keeps for himself. What the Hindu possesses, he is always disposed to share with those who have nothing. In fact, it might be said that a wealthy Hindu considers himself as the depository or distributor, rather than the proprietor of his fortunes, so greatly prone is he to acts of charity and benevolence."

Any one who has mixed with our people, especially away from large cities, would, I think, agree with me when I say, that they are still to a large extent pervaded by the Hindu ideals of self-abnegation and benevolence, and that there is still much less of animality in them than in the corresponding classes in the West. The number of criminals, especially of female criminals in proportion to the total population in India is much less than in the highly civilized countries of the West. I was touring in the Central Provinces during the great famine of 1898-99 and was greatly struck by the patient resignation with which they bore the dire calamity and the benevolent spirit in which they helped one another. There were no riots, no increase in crimes to speak of. There is more poverty here than in the West, and more ignorance judged by the standard of literacy, but there is much less of squalor and brutality, much less of degradation and misery. Our community still produces men of the *statvik* type, though their number is much smaller than before, and they still exert considerable influence upon the other classes. They rarely, if ever, appear in newspaper ; what they do is done in silence and secrecy. While touring in the Rewah State in the nineties of the last century, I was surprised to find that the Gonds of an extensive tract in that state, who, like most other aboriginal tribes, are generally addicted to intoxicating drinks, had given up drinking; and on inquiry, I found out the reason to be the fiat of a *Yogi* who had visited the state sometime before me.

"His order had gone forth from village to village, and the Gonds without question had become total abstainers. No crusade against intemperance could have produced such a wonderful and widespread result. There are no doubt charlatans among the *Yogis* who live upon the credulity of ignorant people. But there cannot be the shadow of a doubt, that there are also genuine men among them, men who devote their lives to spiritual culture in a manner inconceivable to the European."

In regard to the honesty of our people, Sir John Hewet (now Lord Meston), when he was Lieutenant Governor of the United Provinces, said in an interview which he gave to a press-representative :

"In another way the famine (1908, United Provinces) provided an encouraging experience by testifying to the sturdy honesty and self-reliance of the cultivating classes. The Government then advanced nearly a million and a half sterling to cultivators for temporary purposes, in addition to large loans for wells and other permanent additions to irrigation. Practically the whole of this large sum was repaid with the exception of a sum of rather more than £50,000 which had to be remitted owing to the famine being followed by bad seasons in a few small tracts. In one district four thousand individuals took advances for a particular purpose connected with irrigation, and only two were found to have devoted their money to a purpose other than that for which it was intended. The manner in which the people recovered from the disaster that had fallen on them and the punctuality with which the agricultural body repaid their advances seem to me to be the most hopeful augury for the future. I venture to doubt indeed whether *such an experience would be possible in any country but India.*" (The italics are mine).

Intelectual culture.

In regard to intellectual culture, philosophy, the science of language, mathematics, the medical sciences, etc., were carried to a high pitch of development.* When Moslem rule was established over a large part of India Sanskrit science and Sanskrit general literature suffered to a large extent owing to the disappearance of a good number of Hindu courts which patronised them. The last great name the former could boast of was that of Bhascaracharya who wrote his masterpiece, *the Siddhanta Siromani,* about the middle of the 12th century. The last great names in the field of general Sanskrit literature were those of Magha, Sriharsha and Jaydeva, all of whom flourished before the close of the twelfth century. The few courts of Hindu kings, such as that of Bijaynagar in Southern India, which escaped the grasp of the Mahomedans, still fostered Sanskrit learning ; it was also kept up at such places as Benares and Nadia. But during the five centuries and a half of Moslem supremacy Sanskrit literature can boast of only a few commentators, such as Sayanacharya of Bijaynagar, and Raghunandan of Nadia, and Sanskrit seience, of only one astronomer, Raja Jay Singh of Jaipur.

But the loss to Sanskrit literature was more than made up by the gain to the vernacular literatures. It was chiefly the influence of Mahomedanism with its doctrine of the brotherhood of man that produced that succession

*Vide "Epochs of Civilizaton" pp 135–157 and 193-202.

of earnest reformers who shed such lustre on India from the fourteenth century to the sixteenth. Ramananda, Kabir, Nanak, and Chaitanya were certainly influenced by the tenets of Mahomedanism. They all preached the unity of the God-head ; they all protested against caste. They had their disciples not only among the lowest classes of the Hindus, but also among Mahomedans.

The impetus, which the reformers gave, directly and indirectly, to the progress of the vernacular literatures, was very great. In Northern India the teachings of Kabir and Chaitanya were embodied by their followers in voluminous works, which enriched them. They preached to the people in the languages of the people. Their adoption of the vernaculars as their literary languages was a protest against the exclusiveness of the orthodox Brahmans. The books written in Sanskrit were not understood by the mass of the people : they were not meant for the people. Now the people had books written in their vernaculars, books which, if they could not read themselves, they could at least understand if read to them. It was about the time of the Mahomedan Conquset that the Indian vernaculars, the Hindi, the Bengali, the Uriya, and the Marathi, began to be developed. This development was not the direct work of the Mahomedan occupation. Long before that time, even centuries before the Christian era, the mass of the Hindus spoke in Aryan dialects, which were called Prakrits. Varruchi, the earliest Prakrit grammarian, enumerates four classes of these in the sixth century A. D. - Mahárástri, Sauraseni, Mágadhi, and Paisáchi. The vernaculars of India were gradually evolved from these dialects. They must hâve been in process of evolution long before the Mahomedan conquest. But that the first great impulse to vernacular literatures was given by the Vaishnava Reformation which was carried on from the thirteenth to the sixteenth century by Ramananda, Kabir, Chaitanya and a number of other reformers, is shown by the facts that with the exception of some Hindi ballads in Rajputana, vernacular literatures have scarcely anything to shew before the thirteenth century,* and

* The Tamil is excluded from this generalisation. Its development was earlier than that of the other vernaculars. The Tol-kappiyam the oldest extant Tamil work, is believed to have been written a few centuries before the birth of Christ. It is still the greatest authority on Tamil grammar. "Whatever antiquity", says Caldwell, "may be attributed to the Tol-kappiyam, it must have been preceded by many centuries of literary culture. It lays down rules for different kinds of poetical compositions, which must have been deduced from examples furnished by the best authors whose works were then in existence......In endeavouring to trace the commencement of Tamil literature we are thus carried further and further back to an unknown period." ("Comparative

that the earliest writers were mostly Vaishnavas. In northern India, besides the refomer Kabir, the two great Hindi writers previous to the eighteenth century were Sur Das, and Tulsi Das;* and they were both earnest Vaishnavas. The earliest Bengali authors (fourteenth to

---

grammar of the Dravidian Languages," 1875, pp, 127-128). "With the exception of a few works composed towards the end of the twelfth century, nearly all the Telugu works that are now extant appear to have been written in the fourteenth and subsequent centuries, after the establishment of the kingdom of Vijaynagara; and many of them were written in comparatively recent times." (Caldwell *Op, cit.* p. 123). The most ancient and esteemed grammar of classical Canarese, that by Kesava, was written about 1170 A. D, The oldest extant work in Malayalam is "Ramcharita", which was written about the thirteenth Century A. D.

* Sur Das flourished about the middle of the sixteenth century. "He and Tulsi Das" says Mr. Grierson "are the two great stars in the firmament of Indian vernacular poetry. Tulsi was devoted to Ram (*ekant Ram-sebak*) while Sur Das was devoted to Krishna (*ekanta Krishna-sebak*) and between them they are said to have exhausted all the possibilities of poetic art." (Journ. As. Soce. of Bengal pt. I for 1886, special number, p. 21.) Tulsi Das flourished about the commencement of the seventeenth century. For his life see Grierson, *op. cit* p. 42 *et seq*, and Growse's "Ramayana of Tulsi Das", Introduction. In Northern India, the Ramayana of Tulsi Das is "in everyone's hands, from the court to the college, and is read or heard and appreciated alike by every class of the Hindu community, whether high or low, rich or poor, young or old."

the sixteenth century) were enthusiastic worshippers of Krishna, the most notable among them being Bidyapati and Chandi Das. No Marathi writer of any note is known before the thirteenth century and the greatest poets of Maharashtra, Tukaram and Sridhar, were Vaishnavas.*

There was a very wide-spread network of *Pathshalas* (primary schools) for elementary education. Being naturally evolved it was well adapted to the social and economic condition of the people and to their requirements, and maintained by the community it encouraged self-help and self-reliance. Besides, being inexpensive it was capable of very wide extension.

---

* Tukaram died in 1649. He was an ardent worshipper of Vithoba (Vishnu) "He is," says Mr. Acworth, "the most original of all Marathi poets, and his work is remarkable for a high and sustained level of religious exaltation." Sridhar died in 1728. He rendered the Ramayana and the Mahabharata into Marathi. "There is no Marathi poet who equals Sridhar in the acceptance he obtains from all classes. In every town and village in the Deccan and Konkan, especially during the rains, the pious Maratha will be found enjoying with his family, and friends the recitation of the Pothi of Sridhar and enjoying it indeed. Except an occasional gentle laugh, or a sigh, or a tear, not a sound disturbs the rapt silence of the audience, unless when one of those passages of supreme pathos is reached which affects the whole of listeners simultaneously with an outburst of emotion which drowns the voice of the reader." "Ballads of the Marathas" by H. A. Acworth, Introduction.

Sir Thomas Munro had an investigation made into the state of indigenous education in the Madras Presidency. From the results of his inquiries it appears that, in that Presidency, about 1826, the number of schools amounted to 12,493, and the population to 12,850,941, so that there was one school to every thousand of the population, but as only a very few females are taught in schools, we may reckon one school to every 590 of the population.

Arts and Manufactures.

The Fine Arts were carried to a high stage of development as is evidenced by the Buddhist monasteries, chaityas etc., of Bharhut and other places, the magnificent Hindu temples of Srirangam, Madura, Bhubanesvar etc., and the architectural marvels of Northern India like the Taj Mahal.

The Emperor Chandra Gupta had special departments of the state to superintend trade and mining and manufacturing industries. Travellers from Greece, Rome and China marvelled at the skill which the Indians displayed in them. Offerings were made to the gods in the costliest of plate; armour and arms richly decorated with gold and silver, and costly jewellery and dresses of the finest web adorned the persons of the higher classes; and gems, rich brocades, and muslins of the most delicate workmanship found their way from India to the markets of China, Persia, Egypt and Rome. There are references in the Manusamhita to vessels made not only of copper, iron, brass, pewter, tin and lead, but also of gold and silver. Household utensils made of leather, cane, horn, shells and ivory were not uncommon. From the frequent mention of gems and ornaments made of the precious metals as well as from the tax levied upon them, they seem to have been in on small demand. Perfumes, honey, iron, indigo, lac, medical substances, wax, sugar, spice, etc., formed some of the ordinary articles of trade. There are references not only to clothes made of cotton and jute but also to silk and woollen manufactures.

The Hindus made considerable advance in the chemical and metallurgical industries. Varahamihira, who flourished early in the sixth century A.D., mentions several preparations of cements "strong as the thunderbolt," and of dyes, cosmetics and scents. He also refers to mechanical experts. India had already made three important discoveries which for a long time secured her a foremost place in the commercial world—(1) the preparation of fast dyes; (2) the extraction of the principle of indigotin from the indigo plant, and (3) the tempering of steel by advanced metallurgical processes.*

* The remarkable iron pillar near the Kutab Minar at Delhi may be given as an example of the admirable skill of

Indian handicrafts did not suffer from the Mahomedan conquest. Not only did indigenous manufactures flourish under Mahomedan patronage, but many new industries were imported from beyond the confines of India, such as the carpet-weaving of Kurdistan and the glazed pottery of Ispahan. The material condition of the people under the Mogul Empire was, on the whole, one of ease and comfort.

Nicolo-di-Conti, who travelled about A.D. 1420, describes the banks of the Ganges as covered with cities and beautiful gardens. He ascended the Ganges till he come to what he calls a most famous and powerful city named Maurazia abounding in gold, silver and pearls. Baber, who came to India in the beginning of the 16th century, speaks of it as a rich and noble

---

the Hindus. It measures about 24 feet in length, and its diameter is 16 inches at the base and 12 inches at the capital. Its probable date is about the fifth century. "It opens our eyes," say Dr. Fergusson, "to an unsuspected state of affairs to find the Hindus at that age forging a bar of iron larger than any that have been forged even in Europe to a very late date, and not frequently even now. As we find them, however, a few centuries afterwards using bars as long as this Lat in roofing the arch of the temple at Karnak, we must believe, that they were much more familiar with the use of this metal than they afterwards became. It is almost equally startling to find that after an exposure to wind and rain for fourteen centuries, it is unrusted, and the capital and inscription are as clear and as sharp now as when put up fourteen centuries ago."

country, abounding in gold and silver and was astonished at the swarming population, and the innumerable workmen in every trade and profession. Sebastian Manrique, who travelled about 1612, mentions the magnificent cotton fabrics of Bengal exported to all the countries of the East. He describes Dacca, then the capital of Bengal to be frequented by people of every nation and to contain upwards of 200,000 souls. When that town came under British Government its population was also estimated at that figure. Manrique travelled from Lahore to Multan through a country abounding in wheat. rice, vegetables, and cotton. The villages, he tells us, are numerous and contain excellent inns. Tatta in Sind, where he stayed for a month, is described by him to be extremely rich. The country round was of exuberant abundance, particularly in wheat, rice, and cotton, in the manufacture of which at least two thousand looms were employed. Some silk was also produced, and also a beautiful species of leather, variegated with fringes and ornaments of silk. Mandeslo, a German, who travelled about 1638, found Broach to be a populous city, almost filled with weavers, who manufactured the finest cotton cloth in the province of Guzerat. On his way from Broach to Ahmedabad, he passed through Brodera, another large town of weavers and dyers. He was much struck with the splendour and beauty of Ahmedabad, the chief manufactures of which were those of silk and cotton. Cambay appeared to him a larger city than Surat, and carried on an extensive trade. He found Agra, then the capital of India, to be twice as large as Ispahan; a man in one day could not ride round the walls. The streets were handsome and spacious; some were vaulted above for the convenience of shopkeepers, who had their goods exposed there for sale.

Tavernier, who had repeatedly visited most parts of India, says that Shah Jehan reigned not so much as a King over his subjects, but rather as a father over his family and children. He commends the strictness of his civil Government and speaks highly of the security enjoyed under it.

Pictro della Valle, who wrote about 1623, says :—

"Hence, generally, all live much after a genteel way; and they do it securely as well, because the king does not persecute his subjects with false accusations, nor deprive them of anything when he sees them live splendidly."

Bernier, who resided for some time in India about the middle of the 17th century, writes deprecatingly of the wealth of the people. He admits, however, "that India is like an abyss, in which all the gold and silver of the world are swallowed up and lost ; such vast quantities are continually imported thither out of Europe, while none ever returns;" and "that vast quantities of the precious metals are employed not only in earrings, noserings, bracelets of hands and feet, and other ornaments, but in embroidering and embellishing the clothes alike of the Omrahs and of the meanest soldiers."

When Clive entered Murshidabad he wrote of it : "This city is as extensive, populous and rich as the city of London, with this difference that there are individuals in the first possessing infinitely greater property than in the last city."

The transactions of the European trading companies gave great impetus to some of the industries of the sea-board provinces of India. The great silk industry of Bengal, which until a few years ago was in a highly flourishing condition, owed its expansion to the export trade created by the East India Company. The prosperity of the weaving industry of Dacca about the close of the eighteenth century may be best estimated from the fact that, in 1787, fifty lacs of rupees worth of cloths were entered at the Custom House of that town for export to foreign countries.

The indigenous velvets and satins held their own against those imported from abroad. Besides such produce as indigo, spices and sugar, India exported to Europe manufactured cotton and silk. These manufactures must have given employment to numerous artisans. The following are the component parts of the amount of sales by the East India Company in England, reduced to an annual average, in the seventeen years ending 1808-9. *

Piece goods	£1,539,478
Organzine silk	£13,443
Pepper	£195,461
Saltpetre	£180,066
Spices	£112,596
Sugar, Indigo	£272,442
Coffee	£6,624

Muslins and calicoes used to be manufactured in various parts of India, especially in Bengal and the northern part of the coast of Coromandel. Dacca was the chief seat of the muslin manufactures. The Northern Circars and the neighbourhood of Musulipatam were the most distinguished for chintzes, calicoes and ginghams.

General prospeity under Cultural Swaraj.

In regard to the general prosperity under Cultural Swaraj, Abul Fazl says in the *Ain-i-Akberi*:—

"The whole extent of this vast empire is unequalled for the excellence of its waters, salubrity of air, mildness of climate and the temperate constitutions of the natives. Every part is cultivated and full of inhabitants, so that you cannot travel the distance of a Cos (two miles) without seeing towns, and villages, and meeting with good water. Even in the depth of

*H. Murray's "Discoveries and Travels," Vol. II. p. 375.

winter, the earth and trees are covered with verdure ; and in the rainy season, which in many parts of Hindustan commences in June, and continues till September, the air is so delightfully pleasant, that it gives youthful vigour to old age."

The only exception to this general statement noticed by the writer is Bengal. But even there considerable improvement would appear to have been effected during Abul Fazl's time. He says that "for a long time past the air of Bengal had been unhealthy at the leaving off of the rains, afflicting both man and cattle ; but under the auspices of his present Majesty this calamity has ceased."

That until lately the people of the United Provinces and the Punjab enjoyed good health is a well known fact. Allahabad, Agra, Delhi and Lahore were looked upon as sanitaria. Even Bengal was, on the whole, not so fever-stricken, as a large part of it has been since the middle of the last century. "The Dutch Admiral Stavorinus in his Memoirs", says Dr. Bentley, "gives a list of the diseases prevalent in the neighbourhood of Hooghly, but whilst alluding to dysentery and other tropical disorders, he makes no mention of fever or ague. In Valentia's 'Travels' there is no mention of Murshidabad or Berhampore being specifically unhealthy, and some of the early records speak of this part as having once possessed a reputation for salubriousness."*

* "Report on Malaria in Bengal," part I. p. 28.

Towns like Hooghly, Bandel, Chinsura, Baraset, Krishnagar, Burdwan, Midnapur, Pabna, Malda and Birbhum, now hotbeds of malaria, were until about the middle of the last century considered as sanitaria. That despite political revolutions, India was able to maintain her Cultural Swaraj during the earlier years of British Rule is testified to by various writers. Sir Thomas Munro, notwithstanding his natural Western bias declared emphatically, that "If a good system of agriculture, unrivalled manufacturing skill, a capacity to produce whatever can contribute to either convenience or luxury, schools established in every village for teaching reading, writing and arithmetic, the general practice of hospitality and charity amongst each other, and above all a treatment of the female sex full of confidence, respect, and delicacy are among the signs which denote a civilised people—then the Hindus are not inferior to the nations of Europe, and if civilization is to become an article of trade between England and India, I am convinced that England will gain by the import cargo."

CHAPTER III.

DECLINE OF INDIA'S CULTURAL SWARAJ.

I

Cultural subjugation of India.

We saw in the last chapter, that India maintained her Cultural Swaraj and, on the whole, prospered under it down to the earlier years of British Rule. As has been observed by Mr. E. B. Havell, "in the deeper sense India was never conquered. Islam seized her political capitals, controlled her military forces, and appropriated her revenues, but India retained what she cherished most, her intellectual empire, and her soul was never subdued. Her great University cities lost to a great extent their political influence ; some changed their sites as they had often done before ; others, like Benares, Kanchi and Nadiya were less populous and wealthy, but remained as the historic seats of Hindu learning."*

It would perhaps be no exaggeration to say, that the destiny of India in recent times was decided not so much by the result of the battle between Surajudowla and Clive in 1757, as by that of the battle between the Orientalists and the Anglicists in 1835. It has loosened the

* "Aryan Rule in India", p. 408.

bond of cultural affinity and amity which was the strongest that had held together the heterogeneous elements of the Indian nation, and has been fruitful of mischief in various other ways. The battle ground was the Committee of Public Instruction. Until 1834, the heroes in the fight were equally balanced, five against five.

The Orientalists argued, that the education grant of 1813 was assigned for "the revival and improvement of literature," which could only mean oriental literature, and for "the encouragement of the learned natives of India; by which oriental scholars alone could have been intended"; that English education meant only a smattering of it, and the question was between "a profound knowledge of Sanskrit and Arabic literature on the one side, and a superficial knowledge of the rudiments of English on the other," that the classical languages were "absolutely necessary for the improvement of the vernacular dialects" and "that the condemnation of the classical languages to oblivion, would consign the dialects to utter helplessness and irretrievable barbarism," that "little real progress can be made until the learned classes in India are enlisted in the cause of diffusing sound knowledge, and that "one Pundit or Maulavee, who should add English to Sanskrit or Arabic, who should be led to expose the absurdities and errors of his own system, and advocate the adoption of European knowledge and principles, would work a greater revolution in the minds of his countrymen than would result from their proficiency in English alone;" and "that as we have succeeded the native chiefs who were the natural patrons of Indian learning, we are bound to give that aid to oriental scholars which they would have done had they never been displaced by us."

To these arguments, the Anglicists replied, that the grant of 1813 was not only for "the encouragement and improvement of literature and the encouragement of the learned natives of India", "but also for the introduction and promotion of a knowledge of the sciences," by which European sciences alone could be intended, that the example of the Hindu College showed, that Indians could acquire a command of the English language and a familiarity with its literature and science "to an extent rarely equalled by any schools in Europe;" and "the best test of what they can do is what they have done; that all that is required is to impregnate the national mind with knowledge, but by adhering to oriental education the national mind would for ages be kept "in a state of worse than Egyptian bondage, in order that the vernacular dialects may be improved from congenial, instead of from uncongenial sources"; that it was quite unnecessary, even if it was practical, to have able Pundits and Maulvis versed in English to propagate a taste for European knowledge, as such taste had been created already, and the people were greedy for English education; and the English Government were not "bound to perpetuate the system patronised by their predecessors, merely because it was patronised by them, however little it may have been calculated to promote the welfare of the people."

Though the parties were equally balanced, the Orientalists in point of distinction, were at first, the stronger, including as they did among them such men as Wilson and Shakespeare. But the arrival of Macaulay in 1834 and his able advocacy of the cause of the Anglicists turned the scale in their favour; and the discussion was at last terminated by his minute in which he thus sums up his arguments:

"I think it clear that we are not fettered by the Act of Parliament of 1813; that we are not fettered by any pledge expressed or implied; that we are free to employ our funds as we choose; that we ought to employ them in teaching what is best worth knowing; that English is better worth knowing than Sanskrit or Arabic; that the natives are desirous to be taught English, and are not desirous to be taught Sanskrit or Arabic; that neither as the languages of law, nor as the languages of religion, have the Sanskrit and Arabic any peculiar claim to our encouragement; that it is possible to make natives of this country thoroughly good English scholars, and that to this end our efforts ought to be directed."

"In one point I fully agree with the gentlemen to whose general views I am opposed. I feel with them, that it is impossible for us, with our limited means, to attempt to educate the body of the people. We must at present do our best to form a class who may be interpreters between us and the millions whom we govern; a class of persons Indian in blood and colour, but English in taste, in opinions, in morals, and in intellect. To that class we may leave it to refine the vernacular dialects of the country, to enrich those dialects with terms of science borrowed from the Western nomenclature, and to render them by degrees fit vehicles for conveying knowledge to the great mass of the population."

In March 1835, the following resolution evidently determined by the minute of Macaulay was passed by Lord William Bentinck :

"His Lordship is of opinion that the great object of the British Government ought to be the promotion of European literature and science amongst the natives of India, and that all the funds appropriated for the purpose of education would be best employed on English education alone."

It gave immense impetus to English education. Two of the orientalist members of the Committee of Public Instruction tendered their resignation. New members were elected whose views were more in conformity with those of the Government resolution. The Hindus who had hitherto been unrepresented on the Committee were now allowed a share in their deliberations. The newly organised Committee with Macaulay as their President took very active measures for the spread of English education. Six new schools were established the very year the resolution of Bentinck was passed, and six more were established at the commencement of the next year. A library was attached to each school. Books and scientific apparatus of various kinds were ordered from England. Within three years, between 1835 and 1838, the number of seminaries under the control of the Committee rose from eleven to forty, and the number of pupils from about three thousand and four hundred to six thousand.

II

The benefits of English Education.

That the rapid spread of English education has done some good is unquestionable.

It has relaxed the restraints of authority and of conventionalities sanctioned by immemorial usage. Literary ambition has a freer scope, and has been soaring into regions hitherto unknown in India. The Indian intellect has ventured out of the well-beaten paths of theology and metaphysics. The medical and mathematical sciences which yielded such notable results to the ancient Hindus are now being cultivated on the improved methods of the West. Biography, novel (in its modern forms), archaeology, and the different branches of natural science are subjects almost entirely new in modern Indian literature. It is true, the emancipated intellect has been producing much that is worthless and even mischievous, and is marked rather by extent of surface than by depth. In these respects, however, modern Indian literature resembles, to a great extent, its prototype, the Western literature. In the social sphere also many evils which had crept into Hindu Society such as *Sati* and polygamy have been removed.

There is a fable that on the birth of the son of a mighty personage, all the fairies were invited to his cradle except one, and they were all very profuse in their gifts. The uninvited fairy came last in great dudgeon. But unable to reverse what her sisters had done already, she mixed a curse with every blessing they had conferred. From my experience of over six decades, I find the moral of this fable illustrated in most, if not all of our sub-lunary blessings.

Countered by extreme pro-Western bias of the average Neo-Indian

The benefits conferred by English Education are over-whelmingly countered by the evils resulting from the extreme pro-Western bias of the average English-educated Indian or Neo-Indian as he may be conveniently called. He regards the methods and ideals of Western culture to be so superior to those of Indian as to render their propagation to be, on the whole at least, a boon and a blessing, and eagerly pursues the path of Western civilization as the right path of progress and reform. Macaulay had the foresight to predict that English education would train up a "class of persons, Indian in blood and colour, but English in tastes, in opinions, in morals, and in intellect." That is exactly what has happened.

It should be observed, that new India is no longer characterised by that attitude of aggressive hostility which it assumed towards old India in the early years of English education. It was not enough for the first generation of English-educated youths, at least in Bengal, to show their liberation from Hindu superstition by taking beef and drinking spirituous liquors, but some of them went so far as to purposely offend their orthodox neighbours by throwing beefbones into their houses. Happily, new India is now generally free from this pugnacious spirit, and the forces of old India have been gradually increasing in strength. But in this conflict of culture new india is still decidedly the more articulate, if not the stronger factor.

The bias of education, formed at the most impressionable time of life is always very strong and very difficult to remove. The Neo-Indian can hardly be said to have a mind of his own. It is more or less a shadow, a reflection of the Western mind. I find this passage in a work on Indian economics,

Illustrations of this bias.

by a distinguished Indian author, "The rise to a higher standard of life without which no advance in civilization is possible has begun in India."

This is only an echo of the prevailing Western view, that we are just emerging from a lower to a higher state of civilization under Western tutelage. The Western-educated Indian does not pause to ponder whether this "rise" adds to our social efficiency, whether it does not rather diminish it—materially by attenuating to the vanishing point our meagre margin between sufficiency and privation, and morally by inordinately enhancing the stringency of the struggle for animal existence, and thereby leading to the scramble of individual against individual and of class against class, and the consequent diminution of that spirit of benevolence and of social service which has so long cemented our society together, and to various other ethical obliquities. It cannot be gainsaid, that a rise to a higher standard of living is the necessary concomitant of advance in civilization. Such a rise took place in the case of the Hindus as they advanced in civilization some two thousand years ago, and until recently they kept to the standard of decency, comfort and luxury which they then attained. The so called "rise" which is now taking place under the influence of a highly materialistic culture like the modern is only an exchange of the indigenous standard of decency, cleanliness, comfort, and luxury for an exotic one. The exchange, instead of benefiting our community, is, on the whole, doing endless mischief. For instance, in a climate where the minimum of clothing consistent with the indigenous idea of decency, is conducive to health and comfort, the swathing of the body in a multiplicity of cumbersome apparel from head to foot in accordance with the Western idea of decency, produces discomfort, injures health, and drains the purse without any equivalent advantage.

The typical Neo-Indian has become more or less an automaton, moving, acting, and talking much as the Occidental would make him do. He hesitates to take single step for which there is no precedent in the West. He attempts nothing which is not likely to meet with Western approbation, and nothing passes with him which has not the "Hall-mark" of Western approval. He merely echoes the views and shibboleths of the Westerner and does it with all the zeal of a neophyte. The Occidental—naturally enough from his view-point—regards the sparsely clad Indian of simple habits living in the style of his forefathers as but little removed from a barbaric condition. His Indian disciple, as we have just seen, forthwith pleads vehemently for a "rise in the standard of living" after the Western fashion as essential for the emergence of his compatriots from such condition, forces up the demand for drapery and all the tawdry paraphernalia of Western civilization hundredfold, and thus adds fresh links to the ever-lengthening chain of India's industrial slavery and swells the volume of an exhausting economic drain. The Occidental, accustomed to a different state of society and but little acquinted with ours, views, as a rule, the restricted freedom of higher class Hindu females, the comparative seclusion in which they live and their untiring whole-hearted, self-sacrificing devotion to household duties as little better than a state of drudgery and bondage, and unable to reconcile illiteracy with enlightenment, regards them as immersed in darkness. New India at once rings with the cry of the "degraded condition of our womanhood" from end to end; the unregenerate males of old India are reprobated by a hundred tongues and castigated by a thousand pens for perversely keeping their women in a condition of slavery wallowing in the slough of ignorance. That there is room for reform in Hindu Society as there is in every other society goes without saying. But the Neo-Indian reformer knows no way of reform except, that of Western civilization; and burning with zeal he loudly proclaims the gospel of female emancipation on Western lines and girds up to lift the benighted females by making them race with the males along the paths of University education and Western civilization little reflecting upon the goal to which they are likely to lead and to which they are already leading in the West.

The Upanishads were for a long time sealed books to the Neo-Indian. But when a Western philosopher (Schopenhauer) declared emphatically, that "in the whole world there is no study so beneficial and so elevating as that of the Upanishads," and that "it had been the solace of his life, and would be the solace of his death," he began to see that there might really be something in them and to pay them some sort of lip-homage. Vedantism, the most scientific religion which civilized man has risen to as yet, has for good many centuries been, and still is the dominant creed of the enlightened in old India ; but new India knew but little of it until it secured the adherence of Max Muller, Deussen, and other European savants. Even now, the great majority of the Neo-Indians, like the great majority of the

Westerners, look upon Vedantism and similar products of ancient Hindu culture much as they look upon Museum specimens of palœontological and archæological curiosities. The Caste-System is generally regarded by the Westerner as a "monstrous engine of pride, dissension, and shame," and the Neo-Indian, following his lead, anathematizes it and exclaims from house-tops : "Our character is being unhinged, our divisions and dissensions are being sharpened, our activities for public good are being weakened, our very national existence is being threatened by this demon of caste, which has made, and is making cowards of us."

III

Neo-Indian contempt for the ancient culture of India.

The Neo-Indian is so fully convinced of the beneficence of the present system of Education on Western lines, and is so enamoured with it, that he constantly urges its extension in the press and on the platform, for males as well as for females, for the upper as well as for the lower classes. He measures the progress of any particular area, or of any particular section of the population by its progress in literacy on Western methods. The Neo-Indian scholar considers himself so far above the learned of old India, that they evoke in him a complacent feeling of benignant patronage, if not of contemptuous indifference. A discussion at a meeting of the Senate of the Bombay University, held in October, 1913, will illustrate the attitude of new India in this respect. The discussion arose out of the following letter from the Secretary to the Government of Bombay, Education Department, to the Registrar of the University :—

"I am directed to state that at the conference of Orientalists held at Simla in July, 1911, there was a general consensus of opinion that it was necessary while making provision for Oriental study and research on modern critical lines, to maintain side by side with it the ancient and indigenous systems of instruction, since the world of studentship would, it was thought, suffer irreparable loss if the old type of pandit and maulavi were to die out, and that what was needed to promote this indigenous system was encouragement rather than reform. With this object in view it has been suggested that a Sanskrit school might be established at Poona for the training of pandits. The school should be furnished with a good library to which the collection of manuscripts at the Deccan College might be transferred. The students at the proposed school would be partly pandits engaged in the acquisition of Oriental learning on the traditional lines, and partly graduates interested either in Oriental research or in extending their knowledge of the more recondite branches of Oriental studies. The staff would consist partly of the repositories of the ancient traditional learning and partly of modern Oriental scholars. Provision would also be made for the imparting of an elementary knowledge of the English language to the pandit students, and of the German and French languages, a knowledge of which is necessary for the study of modern methods of criticism."

In connection with this letter an elderly Fellow of the Bombay University, who was on the borderland between old and new India, proposed :—

"That Government be informed that the University is prepared to establish a branch of Oriental studies with suitable titles of distinction if arrangements are made for the teaching of this branch of knowledge generally on the lines indicated in the Government letter."

This proposal met with a storm of opposition which was led by a prominent representative of new India. So far as I can gather, his reasons for opposing it are—

First : The traditional mode of learning developed the faculty of "cramming."

Secondly : It was adverse to " liberal education."

"The old traditional learning," said this gentleman "would not stand the test of modern ideas. They should leave the pandits to take care of themselves. If Government desired to give them encouragement let them do so, but the University should have nothing to do with them. He did not want traditional learning at the expense of liberal culture."

Another Neo-Indian gentleman in seconding the amendment said, that:

"He was surprised that at that time of the day they should talk of the preservation of the pandits. Considering the harmful mode of their learning it was not advisable for the University to recognise them by instituting degrees. The University should not extend its recognition to any one who had not acquired an insight into what he called the modern outlook of life. The pandits' outlook of life was so narrow, and the traditional school of learing was so harmful and opposed to modern learning, that by encouraging it they would not be encouraging what was termed liberal education."

Poor pandits ! The fact that such men as Bhaskaracharya, Ramanuja, Ramananda, Madhavacharya, Chaitanya, Rammohan Raya, Isvara Chandra Vidyasagara, Bapudeva Sastri Taracharan Tarkaratna, Sudhakar Divedi, Rakhal Das Nyayaratna and Dayananda Sarasvati have come from their ranks in comparatively recent times – not to speak of the great sages and scientists who flourished during the heyday of our civilization—should have afforded food for reflection to men who have any pretension to "liberal" education. That there are serious defects in the indigenous system of higher education would be readily admitted by all who know anything about it. But it is not so harmful, nor does it compare so very unfavourably with the system of English education in vogue among us, as to be undeserving of the small measure of encouragement vouchsafed by Government. There is I think, no less of "cramming" among us than among the pandits. They exercise their memory to be thorough, we do so merely to pass examinations. Thoroughness and profundity are writ large on the brow of the pandits, as superficiality and shallowness on ours. Then, in regard to the matter "crammed," I am not sure that we can reasonably boast of superior discriminative capacity, when we remember that a good portion of our time has been consumed in committing to memory such things as the feats (with dates) of glorified assassins, murderers, freebooters, and swindlers.

Highly unreasona-alble.

A tree is to be judged by its fruit ; and I have grave doubts if the fruit of the exotic recently planted is so markedly superior to that of the indigenous plant that we can despise it and leave it to perish. The pandit is the embodiment of a high cultural ideal which actuates but few of us. He is but little influenced by commercial considerations. He not only imparts education without any fee but also feeds his pupils ; and though "Brahmacharya" has undergone considerable relaxation of late, the physical and mental discipline they are still subjected to is far more wholesome than what is enforced in our English schools.

Physically, intellectually, and morally the average pandit does not compare at all unfavourably with the average product of English education. I doubt if the pandits as a body are more narrow-minded and illiberal than such sticklers for "liberal culture" as the Neo-Indian scholars who have arraigned them. Lest I should be charged with bias in favour of the pandits, I shall cite the testimony of some Western scholars:

"The Brahmans who compiled," says H. H. Wilson, "a code of Hindu law, by command of Warren Hastings preface their performance by affirming the equal merit of every form of religious worship. Contrarities of belief, and diversities of religion, they say, are in fact part of the scheme of Providence; for as a painter gives beauty to a picture by a variety of colours, or as a gardener embellishes his garden with flowers of every hue, so God appointed to every tribe its own religion, that man might glorify him in diverse modes, all having the same end, and being equally acceptable in his sight. To the same effect it is stated by Dr. Mill in his preface to the Khrista Sangita, or Sacred History of Christ, in Sanskrit verse, that he had witnessed the eager reception of the work by devotees from every part of India, even in the Temple of Kali, near Calcutta, and that it was read and chanted by them with a full knowledge of its anti-idolatrous tendency."*

It would be difficult to find such catholicity and philosophic toleration even now in many parts of the civilized West.

Max Muller thus writes about the pandits:—

"During the last twenty years, however, I have had some excellent opportunities of watching a number of native scholars under circumstances where it is not difficult to detect a man's true character, I mean in literary work and, more particularly, in literary controversy. I have watched them carrying on such controversies both among themselves and with certain European scholars, and feel bound to say that, with hardly one exception, they have displayed a far greater respect for truth, and a far more manly and generous spirit than we are accustomed to even in Europe and America. They have shown strength, but no rudeness; nay I know that nothing

* Essays and Lectures on the Religion of the Hindus, Vol. II. p. 8.

has surprised them so much as the coarse invective to which certain Sanskrit scholars have condescended, rudeness of speech being, according to their view of human nature, a safe sign not only of bad breeding, but of want of knowledge. When they were wrong, they have readily admitted their mistakes; when they were right, they have never sneered at their European adversaries. There have been, with few exceptions, no quibbling, no special pleading, no untruthfulness on their part, and certainly none of the low cunning of the scholar who writes down and publishes what he knows perfectly well to be false, and snaps his fingers at those who still value truth and self-respect more highly than victory or applause at any price. Here too, we might possibly gain by the import cargo. Let me add that I have been repeatedly told by English merchants that commercial integrity stands higher in India than in any other country, and that a dishonoured bill is hardly known there." *

Mr. Adam gives the following interesting description of the pandits :— †

" I saw men not only unpretending, but plain and simple in their manners, and though seldom, if ever, offensively coarse, yet reminding me of the very humblest classes of English and Scottish peasantry; living constantly half-naked and realising in this respect the descriptions of savage life; inhabiting huts which, if you connect moral consequences with physical causes, might be supposed to have the effect of stunting the growth of their minds, or in which only the most contracted minds might be supposed to have room to dwell—and yet several of these men are adepts in the subtleties of the profoundest grammar of what is probably the most philosophical language in existence, not only practically

---

* India : what can it teach us, Lecture II.

† Quoted in F. W, Thomas' History and Prospects of British Education in India, p. 8.

skilled in the niceties of its usage but also in the principles of its structure ; familiar with all the verieties and applications of their national laws and literature and indulging in the abstrusest and most interesting disquisitions in logical and ethical Philosophy. They are, in general, shrewd, discriminating and mild in their demeanour. The modesty of their character does not consist in abjectness to a supposed or official superior, but is equally shown to each other. I have observed some of the worthiest speak with unaffected humility of their own pretensions to learning, with admiration of the learning of a stranger and countryman who was present, with high respect of the learning of a townsman who happened to be absent, and with just praise of the learning of another townsman after he had retired, although in his presence they were silent respecting his attainments"

The pandits have at least preserved the precious heritage bequeathed by our ancestors. But for them much of it would have been irrecoverably lost. Instead of being grateful to them, to load them with contumely, argues a degree of flippancy and narrowmindedness which one would be loath to associate with "liberal culture." Our outlook on life is certainly broader than that of the pandits. But how many of us have either the time or the inclination to inquire whether it is not shallower than of yore? We have learnt to take a brighter view of mundane life than the pandits, but is not much of the brightness the mere shine of flimsy tinsel?

Education is obviously a means to an end. That end is knowledge. But all knowledge is not desirable, as, for instance, the kind of knowledge which enables one to practise robbery or murder more efficiently and more scientifically than he would be able to do without it. From this point of view, the spread of the knowledge of submarines, large, long-range, quickfiring guns, aeroplanes, asphyxiating gases, explosives, &c. is condemnable. Had the Western world been more discriminating and more careful to check the dissemination of such knowledge, it would not have been landed in such a disastrous situation as it is occupying at present. But the Westerners have been under the delusion that the practical applications of physical science to the art of war would make war less frequent and less destructive. The wars of the present century, especially the late World-War have frustrated this expectation, and will, I hope, serve to disillusion them.

Right knowledge, then, is the end of education. But what is right knowledge? There is a certain amount of conflict of opinion between the Ancients and the Moderns in this respect. With the Hindu sages the goal of knowledge was ethical and spiritual advancement. Every system of Hindu philosophy whether theistic, pantheistic, monistic or even agnostic, recognises the salvation of the soul as its end. Its object is to secure the good or well-being of humanity by the development of the inner life for which more or less of abstention from sensual gratification, a life of more or less of ascetic simplicity is requisite. In this respect Hindu culture is at one with the Roman or Greek culture. No Hindu teacher could have exhorted his disciples to be independent of external circumstances and bodily conditions more forcibly or more earnestly than did the Socratic or the Stoic sage. Even Epicurus, with whom pleasure was the sole ultimate good, maintained the immense superiority of the pleasures of the mind over those of the body, and the Epicurean sage no less than the Vedantic sought for happiness and tranquillity of soul from within rather than from without. The ancient philosopher, Eastern as well as Western, strove to keep the struggle for animal existence to the lowest point of animal necessity in order that one might be free, so far as possible, from the moral corruption incidental to it, and might, if he chose, devote more time and energy to the higher and more arduous struggle for spiritual development than he would otherwise be able to do.

The basic principle of modern culture, on the other hand, is to secure the well being of man by perpetually provoking and feeding his sensual desires, by eternally inventing means and appliances for gratifying them. The goal of invention to-day becomes its starting point tomorrow. One effect of this inventional activity has been to commercialise education, especially scientific education—to efface to a very large extent, if not entirely, the old line of demarcation between education for culture and education for livelihood. The technological, that is to say the vocational side of a modern University over-shadows the cultural ; and in countries like Germany, which have taken the lead in modern progress there have sprung up Universities solely for the purpose of technical education. The greatest majority of the scientific men of the present day are only glorified mechanics and tradesmen. The cultured, Ancients, whether in the East or in the West, looked upon trade and industry, in fact all money-making occupations as fit pursuits of people in lower planes. Plato, for instance valued Mathematics only because "it habituates the mind to the contemplation of pure truth and raises us above the material universe." He remonstrated with his friend Archytas who had invented powerful machines on mathematical principles, and declared "this was to degrade a noble intellectual exercise into a low craft fit only for carpenters and wheelwrights." Archimedes was half ashamed of his inventions which were the wonder of his age. Among the Hindus, Manu condemned the institution of huge machinery as a sin. Visvakarma, the divine patron of crafts in India receives worship only from artisans, and he was in no way superior to Maya, the architect of the Danavas. Sukracharya, the greatest Indian inventor of ancient times of whom we have any traditions was a professor of the Daityas.

There is no doubt that the domain of knowledge has been expanding widely and rapidly in the West, but there is equally no doubt that the domain of wisdom has been contracting. Is militarism increasing ? The Westerners set up Hauge Tribunal and League of Nations, while they go on incrcasing their armaments and fiendish means of destruction, feeding greed and sowing discord, and do not make any earnest attempt to curb their grabbing spirit or to promote the spirit of benevolence. Their action is like that of piling faggots on a fire while plying the fire engine, of sprinkling water at the top of a plant while cutting away at its root.

The vast overwhelming mass of Western literature bearing upon an infinity of topics constitutes a gigantic labyrinth in the intricate and bewildering mazes of which one is apt to get lost without any light that would point out a rational goal of his life and help him to attain it. The inventive miracles of the West, however, have enabled it to build up its colossal fabric of industrial civilization and to exploit the weaker peoples of the globe. From the purely material standpoint, therefore it has gained at least temporarily. India, however, has not only not gained but lost heavily. I have elsewhere shown how the spread of Western civilization there has led to physical and moral degeneration. * I propose to show in subsequent chapters how it has adversely affected the industrial fabric of our Cultural Swaraj, annihilated village self-government and created communal conflict. No doubt Government has to a great extent, consciously or unconsciously weakened or destroyed the bulwarks of our Cultural Swaraj. But the Westerners have not yet attained the highest stage of civilization in which selflessness prevails over selfishness. And their prosperity nay, in several cases, even their very existence under existing conditions depends upon the exploitation of the weaker peoples of the globe. But we are perhaps more to blame for having aided and abetted an alien Government with interests and ideals different from and often diametrically opposed to ours.

Indeed, it would, perhaps, be no exaggeration to say, that we have acted like the simpleton of the Sanskrit sloka—

Karastha mudakam tyakta ghanasthama-
bhibanchhati,
Siddhamannam parityajya bhikshamatati
durmati

* "Survival of Hindu Civilization Part 2. Physical Degeneration its causes and remedies," "Some present-day Superstitions" p. p. 240—257.

(The fool neglecting the water at hand aspires to that from the clouds, and despising the ready meal at home goes begging abroad).

CHAPTER IV

THE DESTRUCTION OF VILLAGE SELF-GOVERNMENT.

I

Political aspiration of New India for the Western form of democracy

English education first initiated the Indian into a historical literature which showed how the people had come to be a great political power among several of the most civilized nations of the West ; how they had wrested important privileges from unwilling tyrants ; how they had risen against despots, deposed them, nay even executed them and established republican forms of government.

Writing as early as 1838, twenty years after the establishment of the first English school in Bengal, Sir C. Trevelyan recognised in the educated youth of that province a strong desire for representative form of Government. Some of his observations in this connection are so suggestive and are made in such a sympathetic spirit that they may be aptly quoted here. Coming from the North-Western province to Bengal, he was struck by the remarkable difference in the political attitude of the better class people in the two provinces. In the former, where English education had scarcely penetrated yet, the people had no other idea of political betterment than the absolute expulsion of the English ; in Bengal, on the other hand, where English education had already made some progress, some form of representative national assembly was held up as the ideal. "No doubt, both the schemes of national improvement (the sudden and absolute expulsion of the English, and the gradual formation of national representative assembly)," says Trevelyan, "suppose the termination of the English rule ; but while that event is the beginning of the one, it is only the conclusion of the other. In one, the sudden and violent overthrow of our Government is a necessary preliminary ; in the other, a long continuance of our administration, and the gradual withdrawal of it as the people become fit to govern themselves, are equally indispensable." *

With the progress of English education, the idea of representative government has taken deep root into the Indian mind. It has been fostered not only by the spirit of English literature with its Milton, Burke and Mill, but also by the living sympathy of a few noble-minded Britons like George Thompson, Allan O. Hume and Sir William Wedderburn who have cordially helped or guided the political

* Trevelyan, *On the Education of the people of India*, (London, 1838) p, 200.

aspirations of educated Indians. Political Associations sprang up as a consequence, such as the British Indian Association of Bengal, the Puna Sarvajanik Sabha of Bombay and the Mahajana Sabha of Madras. These provincial movements were centralised in 1885 by the National Congress which brought the political aspirations of new India to a focus.

All this political activity is quite natural. It is but natural that when one suffers from what he considers to be wrongs he should give as emphatic an expression to them as is possible. Apart from the useful social purpose served by the National Congress by bringing together a fair number of the representatives of the educated community from all parts of India and enabling them to mix together and interchange their ideas, authoritative pronouncements on current political subjects by such a representative assembly have unquestionably had some effect. But its importance and usefulness have been greatly over-estimated, and the belief that it will ever lead to anything like the "system of Government similar to that enjoyed by the self-governing members of the British Empire" is, as we shall see hereafter, altogether illusory. What little of redundant energy there is in new India, finds its vent chiefly in political activity. The men who, in the estimation of new India, are building up an Indian "nation" are, almost without exception, men who are distinguished for such activity. To be able to make eloquent speeches on political platforms has hitherto been the highest aspiration of the average Neo-Indian outside Government service. The consequence is, an amount of energy has been expended upon politics which is altogether disproportionate to its import in national life, and incommensurate with the results obtained. Not only so : a portion of the energy has been directed to dangerous paths, dangerous alike to those who pursue them and to the entire community.

Leads to disregard of indigenous democracy.

Probably the most serious injury which the slave mentality of New India has done to the cause of the Indian nation is its utter disregard of the indigenous form of democracy, the village Self-Government, which from time immemorial was the basis of Indian polity. As has been observed by Mr. E. B. Havell, "it was a scheme of communal village life, worked out by the practical philosophy of one of the most highly gifted of the races of mankind, in which each section of the community and each individual member of it took their allotted shares of work for the common weal, not under the compulsion of an autocrat or of a ruling caste, but by a clear perception of mutual advantage, and a voluntary recognition of superior intellectual leadership."

According to the *Sukraniti*, "The kings troops were not to be quartered upon villagers, and his officers and servants were not to live in the villages, nor meddle in their affairs. No soldier was to enter a village except with a royal permit, nor was he in any case to oppress villagers. The village headman, as the king's deputy should be a father and mother to the people', and protect them "from bandits, thieves and officials." "For who" says Sukracharya, "does not get intoxicated by drinking the vanity of office ?"

"While the rights of the village communities were thus jealously safeguarded, the principle of self-government also extended to craft guilds, banking and mercantile corporations and religious organisations. The King's courts did not interfere in their domestic affairs : all disputes between members were settled according to custom and the traditions of each of these bodies, because such disputes involved technical questions upon which the King's officers could not properly adjudicate." *

"So far as archaeological research has gone the period which yields the most interesting records relating to the constitution and powers of the village Assemblies is from the time of Sankaracharya down to A. D. 11 00, though there is no reason to doubt that such institutions existed in much earlier times and were part and parcel of the Aryanisation of the South. These inscriptions, mostly inscribed on the walls of the temple mandapams which formed the local Council Chambers and town halls, show that the same system of village unions under the control of a King's officer which existed in the days of Chandragupta Maurya was maintained in Southern India in mediaeval times. But the point which the *Kautilya Artha Sastra* does not bring out is the great extent of the powers exercised by the local Assemblies—the Sabhas and Mahasabhas—and the extreme respect paid to the 'great men' of the village by the officers of the king.

* E. B. Havell "Aryan Rule in India pp. 48-49."

Even when the King's intervention in the affairs of the village union is invoked, the edict of the Assembly which settles a dispute is not issued in the King's name, but in that of the "great men" to whom the royal envoy himself applies the honorific form of address, 'their majesties'.

These village parliaments though responsible to the supreme Government for the payment of the taxes due from village lands had complete control over the collection of them and the lands not reserved as royal domains or dedicated to religious purposos belonged ultimetly to the Assembly, not to the State." *

Testimony of English officials to the vitality of village Self-Government

Village self-government was the one vital thing in the country which not only kept society together but made it prosperous despite the divisions of caste and despite the occasional misrule of tyrannically and viciously disposed despots, whether Hindu, Buddhist or Mahomedan. The Central Government might be dead and rotten to the core, but that did not seriously affect the life of the people whose soul lay in the villages. This is abundantly shown by the testimony of high English officials during the earlier years of British Rule.

"The Municipal and village institutions, of India," says Sir J. Malcolm, "are competent from the power given them by the common assent of all ranks in the country, to maintain order and peace within their respective circles......

"As far as we can trace the history of Central India their rights and privileges have never been contested, even by the tyrants and oppressors who slighted them ; while, on the other hand, all just princes have founded their chief reputation and claim to popularity on attention to them."

* E. B. Havell "Aryan Rule in India," p. 228.

"In whatever point of view we examine the Native Government in the Deccan," says Elphinstone, "the first and most important feature is the division into villages or townships. These communities contain in miniature all the materials of a state within themselves, and are almost sufficient to protect their members, if all other Governments are withdrawn." After mentioning the defects of Mahratta Rule he says :

"But with all these defects, the Mahratta country flourished, and the people seem to have been exempt from some of the evils which exist under our more perfect government. There must therefore have been some advantages in the system to counterbalance its obvious defects, and most of them appear to me to have originated in the fact, that the Government although it did little to obtain justice for the people left them the means of procuring it for themselves. The advantage of this was particularly felt among the lower orders who are most out of reach of their rulers, and most apt to be neglected under all governments. By means of the Panchayat they were enabled to effect a tolerable dispensation of justice among themselves."

Lieut. Col. Mark Wilks says, "Each Hindu township is, and indeed always was, a petty republic by itself. The whole of India is nothing more than a vast congeries of such republics." "The village communities," says Sir C. Metcalfe, "are little republics having nearly everything they can want within themselves and almost independent of any foreign nation. They seem to last when nothing else lasts. Dynasty after dynasty tumbles down ; revolution succeeds revolution ; Pathan, Mughal, Maratha, Sikh and English are all masters in turn ; but the village communities remain the same. In times of trouble they arm and fortify themselves, hostile army passes through the country, the village communities collect their cattle within their walls and let the enemy pass unprovoked. If plunder and devastation be directed against themselves and the force employed be irresistible, they flee to friendly villages at a distance; but when the storm is over they return and resume their occupations. A generation may pass away, but succeeding generation will return.

This union of the village communities each one forming a separate little state in itself, has. I conceive, contributed more than any other course to the preservation of the people of India through all the revolutions and changes which they have suffered, and is in high degree conducive to their happiness, and to the enjoyment of a great portion of freedom and independence."

Sir Thomas Munro says. "It appears that under the Hindu administration there were no courts of Justice excepting the cutchery of the *patails* and *amildars* and that all civil cases of importance were settled by Panchayets...... The native who has a good cause always applies for a Panchayet, while he who has a bad one seeks the decision of a collector or a judge because he knows it is much easier to deceive them. The natives cannot surely, with any foundation be said to be judged by their own laws, while the trial by Panchayet to which they have always been accustomed is done away......I conscientiously believe that for the purpose of discriminating the motives of action and the chances of truth in the evidence of such a people the entire life of the most acute European judge devoted to that single object eould not place him on a level with an intelligent Hindu Panchayet which is an admirable instrument of decision."

The condition of Central India during the administration of Sir J. Malcolm, afforded him a good opportunity of judging how far Panchayets could be employed in the difficult system of British Government.

"The result of the experiment," says Malcolm, "was satisfactory. When any of the subjects of the princes and chiefs under British protection had disputes regarding land or property demanding our mediation, the aid of a Panchayet was invariably resorted to, and its opinion made the guide for a decision. The knowledge and discrimination which some of the members displayed on the trial, and the distinctness of the grounds on which the court made up its judgment were surprising. There was in no instance any cause to suspect these courts of partiality, much less of corruption...... Many complaints brought before the local officers were withdrawn, when submitted to a Panjayet. This happened when the complainant knew himself unable to substantiate the charges ; and men who had advanced false claims or accusations, continually came forward, after the Panchayet had assembled, and sometimes when its proceedings were advanced, with a written acquittal (Razeenama) of those they had desired to injure, which, where the case was not criminal, was always deemed sufficient. The frequent occurrence of the latter instances was considered as a proof that Native Panchayet courts must, from their constitution, prevent litigation, as they offer, to him who is conscious of wrong, none of those hopes of escape which present themselves under a system where the forms are more unbending, where pleaders have more art, and the judges (however superior in principle and general ability) have a less minute knowledge of the cunning, the shifts and evasions of those brought before him."

"With no advocates, solicitors, or other blood-suckers now become necessary adjuncts of a court of justice in Europe", says Abbe Dubois, "the Hindus determined the greater part of their suits of law by the arbitration of friends or of the heads of caste, or in cases of the very highest importance, by reference to the chiefs of the whole castes of the district assembled to discuss the matter in controversy".

The saddest, the most tragic fact in the history of India is that of the annihilation of

Extinction of village Self-Government the greatest wrong under British Rule

the village self-government. The killing of the village organism is the cruellest wrong which the British Government, consciously or unconsciously, has done to India. It is a grievance compared to which such grievances as the inadequate representation of our educated community in the Imperial Services, civil as well as military, the union of the judicial and executive services, the Arms Act, the Press Act &c., dwindle into utter insignificance, are mere bagatelles, yet hardly any voice is ever raised about it. The leaders who speak in the name of the people of India do not appear to be aware of the greatest wrong which they have suffered under the British regime. The philanthropic patriots of new India generally profess to be inspired by the noble idea of effecting a blend between Indian and Western civilizations. But they appear to be so obsessed by Western prepossessions that what they fondly believe to be a blend is often characterised by the almost utter absence of the Indian element.

It is much to be doubted whether the Western form of ballot-box Democracy is superior to the Indian. The former is barely a century old, and it is already showing signs of disintegration and reversion to autocracy and dictatorship in various countries such as Italy, Spain, Greece and Jugo-Slavia.

The structure of Self-Government on the Western model which New India aspires to appears to us to have hardly any foundation in reason, certainly not in the experience, the traditions, and the sentiments of the Indian people. No wonder it has been such an egregious failure. And it will continue to be a failure unless and until it is based upon the indigenous system traces of which are still to be met within old India. Not only has New India looked askance at the demolition of indigenous democracy, but aspiring to representative central Government after the Western fashion, the leaders of new India even took an active part in the demolition of the rural "republics" which made the people to a large extent independent of the central Government. The judicial function was one of the most important of the functions exercised by the village Panchayet. There is no doubt that the British machinery for the administration of justice is, as a machine, much more advanced. But sociological advance from simplicity to complexity is good only within limits to be determined by economic and ethical considerations. Even in a superlatively rich country like England, the system of administering justice is strongly condemned as too costly, too dilatory, too aleatory and too complex by Herbert Spencer and other thinkers. How much more must the evils be in a country like

India, where the margin between sufficiency and starvation is extremely narrow, and where, besides, the administration of justice is to no small extent carried on by foreigners but little acquainted with the customs and idiosyncrasies of the people. Yet, not only has no systematic attempt worth the name been made to check the progress of a system which is daily causing such havoc, both moral and economic, around us, but its extension is often welcomed and even pleaded for.

Within half a century between 1877 and 1927, the stamp revenue has in round figures increased from about three crores to thirteen. But the population of British India has within that period increased from about 191 millions to only 247 millions. The enormous augmentation of the stamp Revenue represents only a fraction of the extent to which the people are increasingly exploited by the expansion of the British judiciary. The number of Neo-Indians subsisting by the legal profession increased in two decades from 251,608 in 1901 to 336, 510 in 1921. Their earnings are very unequal ranging from about two lakhs to two hundred rupees a year. Taking the annual average to be five hundred rupees, the legal profession must absorb some sixteen crores a year.

If to this be added the stamp revenue (making due allowance for revenue from nonjudicial stamps) and the incidental expenses upon witnesses, *amlas* &c., the aggregate amount of the legal exploitation of the Indian people would probably not fall short of twenty-five crores a year. This is an exorbitant price to pay for such justice, or rather such law as is administered by the Law Courts. A part of it is no doubt paid by men who can well afford it. But the greater portion is wrung out of men in whose case it means so much subtraction from the narrow margin between sufficiency and want or starvation.

In justice to the Government it should be said, that there were large-hearted sympathetic administrators in the earlier years of British Rule, men like Munro, Elphinstone and Malcolm, who recognised the value of the self-governing rural institutions and tried to keep them up. But they failed. The failure was due to various causes—ignorance, want of confidence in the people, non-settlement of the land revenue with village communities where such communities existed, bias in favour of the English Judicial system. Hastings admitted that the assumption of the entire criminal jurisdiction of the country by Government was a "usurpation, but they could not avoid it......they would have had clashing powers." The latest instance of the extinction of village self-Government is furnished by Upper Burma, and I shall let an English official, an experienced member of the Civil Service, say how it has been effected :

"The English Government on taking over Upper Burma recognised the extreme value of this organisation. In lower Burma much of our difficulty arose from the fact that the organisation was wanting, and that between Government and the individual there was no one. So one of the first efforts of Government in Upper Burma was to endeavour to preserve and strengthen this local Self-Government. Unfortunately every effort it made resulted in destroying it rather than consolidating it. A wrong view was taken from the beginning.

The council was ignored. How this happened I do not know. I can only suppose that it arose from ignorance. The only man recognised by the Burma Government we replaced was the headman. They dealt directly with him and not with the council. They did not appoint the council or regulate it in any way. In law no council existed. Therefore, when we took over, the law was mistaken for the fact—a common mistake, due to seeking for knowledge in papers, and not in life,—and the council was ignored. The following seems to have been the argument :

Government appointed the headman, therefore he was an official. Government did not appoint or recognise any council, therefore there was no council. Any how, that was the decision arrived at and enforced.

There is on record a circular of the Local Government in which the headman of a village is described as a Government Official ; to be to his village what the District Officer is to his district. That is disastrous. A headman is not an official of the Government. His whole value and meaning is that he is a representative of the people before Government. He expresses the collective views of the villages and receives the orders of Government for them as a whole. He is their head, not a finger of Government. He corresponded almost exactly to the mayor of an English town, who would be insulted if you called him a Government Official. Yet this mistaken view was taken of the village headman, and this error has vitiated all dealings of Government with the village organisation and its headman. He is appointed by Government instead of being appointed by the people and approved by Government. He is responsible to Government, not to his village,—as he ought to be—for the use or abuse of his powers. He is punished by Government for laxity. By the Village Regulation he can be fined by the District Officer.

There has grown up among Europeans in the East a custom of imposing fines. They fine their servants for breakages and innumerable other small matters, and then complain how scarce good servants are. The clerks in Government offices used to be subject to continual fines until Lord Curzon stopped it. Now, headmen of villages can be fined by the District officer ; and they are fined ; the proviso is no dead letter. It is a mark of the "energetic" officer to use it. Can there be anything more destructive ? Imagine the headman. the mayor of a community of three or four thousand people, fined five shillings for the delay of a return, or set, like a school boy, to learn a code—with the clerks. I have seen this done often. What respect for Government, what from his own people, what self-respect, can he retain after such treatment ?

Again by ignoring the council and making the headman an official, Government set up a number of petty tyrants in the villages, free from all control but its own ; consequently it has been forced to allow great latitude of appeal. This still further destroys his authority. He is under old custom, legalised by the village Regulation, empowered to punish his villagers who disobey him in certain matters. The punishments are, of course, trivial. When approved by the council, as in old days, they were final ; but now they can be appealed against—and are. A headman who endeavours to enforce his authority runs the risk of being complained against and forced to attend Headquarters, to waste days of valuable time and considerable sums of money to defend himself for having fined a villager a shilling for not mending his fence. One or two experiences of this sort and the headman lets things slide in future.

Thus interference with the village is constant and disastrous. Headmen are bullied, fined, set to learn lessons like children, all in the name of efficiency. And Government wonders why the village system decays. A continual complaint of Government is that headmen are no longer the men they used to be, that they have lost authority. The best men will not take the appointment—and who can wonder ? Here is a story in illustration :

There was a small village in my district, on a main road, and the headman died. It was necessary to appoint a new one. But no one would take the appointment. The elders were asked to nominate a man, but no one would take the nomination. I sent the Township Officer to try to arrange ; he failed.

Now a village can not get along without a headman. Government is at an end ; no taxes can be collected, for instance ; therefore it was necessary a headman be appointed at once. I went to the village myself and called the elders and gave them an order that they must nominate some one. So next morning, after stormy meetings in the village a man was brought to me and introduced as the headman-elect. He was dirty, ill-clad, and not at all the sort of man I should have cared to appoint, nor one whom it would be supposed the villagers would care to accept, yet he was the only nominee.

"What is your occupation ?" I asked.

He said he had none.

"What tax did you pay last year ?" I asked him this in order to discover his standing, for men are rated according to their means.

He told me that he had paid five shillings less than a third of the average.

"You are willing to be headman ?" I asked.

"No," he said frankly. "But no one would take the place, and the elders told me I must. They said they would prosecute me under the 'bad livelihood' section if I didn't. I could take my choice between being headman or a term in prison."

This was, of course, an extreme case, but it illustrates the position. The headman is degraded and all administration suffers."*

Recent re-establishment of so-called village Self-Government not calculated to be beneficial.

Efforts have been made within the last decade to re-establish village self-government. But the following observations which I made in regard to the Bengal Village Self-Government Bill in the Modern Review (June, 1918) apply to them generally in all parts of India.

"It is undoubtedly necessary that Government should exercise a certain amount of control over the village committees. But self-government to be successful must be real, and the control should be so exercised that the committees may feel it as little as possible, and that their sense of responsibility may not be impaired. Too much supervision, too many rules and regulations, and too rigid observance of these would deprive them of the amount of freedom, initiative, prestige and responsibility which is essential for the success of the measure.

The Dafadars and Chaukidars will be the most important, if not the only servants of the village. They are, of course,

* "The Passing of Empire'' by H. Fielding Hall,—pp. 138—141.

to be controlled by the village committee, and are enjoined to obey its orders in regard to keeping watch in the village, and in regard to other matters connected with their duties (clauses 22 and 26 ix). These duties, however, are prescribed (clause 26) in such a manner that they could be performed independently, without any reference whatever to the committee. Their allegiance would apparently be divided between three masters—the nearest police officer, the circle officer (representing the District Magistrate), and the village committee. And as their appointment, punishment, and dismissal, and the determination of their pay and equipment would rest with the officials (clauses 23, 24 and 25), it is not difficult to predict whom they would try to please and who would really control them. The 'self-government' of the village committee would thus become a highsounding, solemn sham. No capable, self-respecting man would desire the position of a 'master' who has but nominal authority over his servants.

Maximum of authority and minimum of control should be the fundamental principle of genuine local self-government. The village committee, however, has, as we have just seen, been entrusted with the minimum of authority, and has, as we shall presently see, been burdened with the maximum of control, and control too of a most undesirable character. The control is vested partly in the circle officers and partly in the District Magistrate. In both cases it would practically be in the hands of the circle officers, who are, I believe, usually, if not invariably, young Sub-Deputy Magistrates. This conclusion is confirmed by Sir Satyendra Prasanna Sinha's statement 'that it is intended that the new system should be introduced gradually in districts where the circle system has been introduced, and circle officers are available to assist the village committee.' The 'assistance' would virtually mean control. Man, as ordinarily constituted, is fond of the exercise of power ; and the younger and more energetic he is, the more marked is this fondness. Actuated by it, if not, in some cases, by any baser motive, the Sub-Deputies and possibly also the Sub-Inspectors of the nearest police stations, to whom also the Chaukidars and Dafadars would be partly subordinate, would, I have but little doubt, often needlessly meddle with the work of the village committees and hamper it. In fact the 'assistance' would, I am afraid, be often rendered in such a manner as to make the village committee the lowest and the most subservient link of the official chain, and 'self-government' a farce. An exceptionally broad-minded, sympathetic, energetic and experienced District Magistrate would no doubt keep his subordinates in check. But such officers are rare. Besides, under the present system of administration, the man is generally swallowed up in the machine, and even the best of district officers would not have much scope for freedom and initiative. For, cut and dry rules would be framed by Government 'regulating the powers and duties of village committees in regard to sanitation, conservancy, drainage, buildings, roads, bridges and water-supply,' and 'in regard to schools and dispensaries,' etc. (clause 111, 2i), and the function of the district officers would be to see that the rules are observed—a function which would be usually performed by their subordinates the Sub-Deputies."

"Government proposes to overcome 'the evils which menace health and life' and which have been gradually growing in enormity and intensity by the expansion of the Sanitary Department so that the Sanitary Commissioner may have 'a large executive agency' to see that the 'model rules of village hygiene' framed by Government are carried into practice. And the money required for 'the sanitation, conservancy, drainage and water-supply of the village, for the establishment, repair, maintenance or management of primary schools and dispensaries, for any other local works likely to promote the health, comfort, and convenience of the public,' as well as 'for the salaries and equipment of the Dafadars and Chaukidars, and the salary of the Secretary (if any),' is to be raised by taxing the villagers (clause 38 of the Bengal Village Self-Government Bill).

It is not difficult to predict, that in the great majority of cases, especially if the principles underlying the Bengal bill be applied to all other parts of India, this method of financing the proposed Village Committees would be productive of great hardship, would, in fact, lead to increased impoverishment and consequent further decrease of vitality and aggravation of the evils which menace health and life."

CHAPTER V

PASSING OF COMMUNAL CONCORD

I

Former Hindu Moslem amity—an illustration

In Chapter I we saw how amicable relation was gradually established between Hindus and Mahomedans. The following anecdote from the life of the great saint and reformer Chaitanya may be given as an illustration.

There was a party among the orthodox Hindus of Nadiya who were averse to his not making any distinction of caste and creed among his followers and to his Kirtans in the streets (singing of hymns to the accompaniment of drums and cymbals). They complained to the Mahomedan Governor of Nadiya, Chand Kazi, and asked him to stop the Kirtans, which were accordingly prohibited. On being informed of this, Chaitanya collected his followers one evening. Many Kirtan parties were formed each with two drums and a dozen singers. The procession marched towards the house of the Governor who ordered his soldiers to stop it. They, however, failed to do so, and as the crowd came to the house of the Governor, he took refuge in the inner apartments. "He came out, however, on being assured that he had nothing to fear. Nimai (Chaitanya) received him with the honour due to his position and addressed him thus: "How is it *mamu* (uncle) that in coming to your house, you instead of giving me a welcome, tried to hide yourself?" The Governor replied "You see, nephew, I had given you offence and when you arrived, I saw that your people were bent upon revenge. So what could I do but avoid their presence? Now as it seems you have forgiven me, I have come out without hesitation to welcome you." To which Gauranga (Chaitanya) rejoined: "I have to ask you one question: kindly reply frankly. Why did you stop my Kirtan which is only a way of worshipping the deity? You may not like it, but why should you not permit others to worship the Lord in the way they think best, especially when there is nothing objectionable or immoral in it? The Kazi replied: "I fully agree with you. Then let me tell you the whole history...... It is not my fault that I objected to the Kirtan. The leading Hindus of the town came to me to complain against you and your method of worship ..... And it was then that I was led to take action." Chaitanya then requested the Kazi to cease meddling with the Kirtans. The Kazi replied with warmth: "Stop Kirtan again ? No I shall never do so. But I will do this. I shall leave a legacy to my heirs for the protection of Kirtan. My curse be over their heads if they ever meddle with it." The Kazi's grave exists in Nadiya. It is held in great veneration by the followers of Sri Chaitanya. Whoever goes on pilgrimage to Nadiya takes care to visit the grave and salute it." *

From this anecdote, we find how cordial the relationship between Hindus and Mahomedans was. The Mahomedan Governor used to call Chaitanya's father "brother." Hence Chaitanya addressed him as uncle. We can hardly conceive of a district officer of the present day responsible for law and order maintaining it in the way the Kazi did. Had there been the "music before mosque" bogy in Chaitanya's time he and his followers could not have conducted their Kirtan all over Bengal during the reign of a Mahomedan King. The truth is, the charge of intolerance against the Mahomedan rulers of India has but a slight foundation in fact. Invaders like Mahmud of Ghazni, who had no permanent interest in the country, might plunder and destroy. But the policy of those, who, after Mahomed Ghori, settled and ruled in India, was different. They compare very favourably, indeed, with the contemporary Christian monarchs of Europe.

---

* Sisir Kumar Ghose's "Lord Gauranga" Vol. I.

The persecution of Jews by Christians, of one Christian sect by another, of the Protestants by the Roman Catholics, of the Roman Catholics by the Protestants, of one section of the Protestants by another in Christian Europe, was on the whole incomparably severer than that of the persecution of the Hindus by their Musalman rulers in heathen India. The horrors of the inquisition were here unknown, except, perhaps, in a small territory ruled by the Roman Catholics. Khafi Khan, himself a bigot, was shocked by the intolerant conduct of the Europeans of his day in India, (commencement of the 18th century). Speaking of those settled in Hugli, he says ; "of all their odious practices this was the worst :—in the port which they occupied in the sea-coast, they offered no injury either to the property or person of either Mahomedans or Hindus who dwelt under their rule ; but, if one of those inhabitants died leaving children of tender age, they took both the children and the property under their charge, and whether these young children were *Sayids*, or whether they were Brahmans, they made them Christians and slaves (*Mamluks*)" *

* It is doubtful whether the cruelties perpetrated by the Portuguese at Salsette were equalled by the most fanatical and insensate Moslem that ever ruled in any part of India. A Portuguese armament landed at Salsette when least expected,

The Mahomedan author of *Seir Mutaqherin* justly observes that "the inhabitants of India have been constantly subdued by foreign conquerors, and vanquished by foreign armies. But so tenacious were the vanquished of their own tenets and customs, that the victors soon found themselves under the necessity of assimilating with them; and so soon as these mighty conquerors acquired a firm footing in these countries, and the violence and extortions inseparable from a state of warfare and slaughter and confusion came to be over, their first thought was always to quiet the minds of the inhabitants, and to afford them relief, by always becoming their protectors in whatever concerned their lives, fortunes, honor and families. In consequence of such administration on one side and such sentiments on the other, the country was populous and flourish-

---

and carrying all before them, destroyed 1200 temples with all their images." A new expedition was fitted out soon after, which landed as before, "and not only destroyed the temples, but set fire to the cities, villages and all the habitations, and in a few hours reduced the whole island to ashes. The affrighted inhabitants fled almost naked from their houses and sought shelter on the shore of the neighbouring continent; and this scene of culture and crowded population, was converted at once into a smoking desert. Father Berno followed the troops, wielding a huge club, with which he beat down all the idols and broke them in pieces." Murrays Discoveries and Travels in Asia" p. 78

ing beyond imagination; and the inhabitants contented and happy, as well as sincere."

Present day Hindu Moslem antgonism.

The amicable relations between Hindus and Mahomedans lasted till about the closing years of the last century. During the last two or three decades, however, these relations have been severely strained, and discord now prevails where formerly there was concord. Embittered and widespread antagonism between the Hindus and the Mahomedans is the most distressing feature of Indian society at the present day. More or less serious affrays between them have of late become very common in some part or other of India. "Forty riots took place during the twelve months ending with April 1st 1927, resulting in the deaths of 197 persons and in injuries more or less severe to 1,598 others. These disorders were widespread, but Bengal, the Punjab, and the United Provinces were the parts of India most seriously affected. Bengal suffered most from rioting, but on many occasions during the year tension between Hindus and Mahomedans was high in the Bombay Presidency, including its outlying division, Sind."*

Innumerable conferences have been held recently for remedying this lamentable state of affairs. The most important of these was the Unity Conference held at Delhi in Septem-

* "India in 1926-27", p. 2.

ber, 1924. It was inaugurated by twenty one days' fast which Mahatma Gandhi imposed upon himself as vicarious penance for the recent regrettable intensity of Hindu-Moslem conflict, and drew the sympathy and benediction not only of all the articulate sections of Indian communities (Hindu, Mahomedan, Buddhist, Christian and Parsi) but also of cultured foreigners (including high officials of Government). It sat for a week and was largely attended by representatives from all parts of India. But, it proved a failure like the conferences which had preceded it and those which have succeeded it. The President of the Conference, Pandit Motilal Nehru, pointed out that "meetings of Hindus and Musalmans had been held all over the country, and resolutions passed during the last few years", but "all that was done during the last twenty years had come to nothing," despite the fact that Hindu-Moslem Unity has long been one of the chief planks of the Indian National Congress. Earnest impassioned exhortations for communal concord are punctuated by pathetic jeremiads on communal discord.

The immediate causes of the recent Hindu-Moslem riots are of a most frivolous description. The fact of the matter is, that when people are predisposed to quarrel, they would never be at a loss to find a pretext for it.

Conferences of high-souled and broad-minded philanthropists for delivering homilies on toleration, and for regulating Hindu processions before mosques, *Namaz*, Arati, cow-slaughter etc., would be of little avail. To compare small things with great, there have been no end of peace-conferences in Europe beginning with the Hague, but militarism has been growing apace during the last three decades, and Europe just now may not inaptly be described as a vast military camp. The truth is, as in the one case so in the other, the one thing which is essential for enduring peace, without which peace-conferences are useless, and with which they are superfluous, is benevolence. That however, is not only wanting, but as we shall presently see, present conditions are as unfavourable to its growth, as they are favourable to the growth of malevolence.

The Hindus in self-defence have started the Hindu Maha Sabha as a reply to the Moslem League; and the *Suddhi* and *Sangathan* movements of the Hindus have been replied by the *Tanzin* and *Tablegh* movements of the Moslems.

II

Causes of the Hindu-Moslem conflict:

We have seen in chapter I, that fundamentally the foundation of the amity which formerly prevailed among the Hindus and the Mohamedans was cultural. Its recent diminu-

1. Supersession of Indian by Western Culture.

tion to almost vanishing point at places, appears to us to be primarily attributable to the undermining of that foundation by the multitudinous forces of the modern culture of the West. Natural Science is the intellectual foundation of this culture, as mental science is that of ancient culture whether Hindu or Mohamedan.

The ancients subordinated science to philosophy. The moderns, on the other hand, elevate science above philosophy. The modern scientists would practically resolve all knowledge into sensations, would not admit anything which is not susceptible of experimental demonstration and scrupulous verification, would exclude the ultra-sensual region from their purview altogether, and any scientist like Oliver Lodge or Russell Wallace, who ventures to pry into it, is hooted as a renegade. The ancient philosophers, on the other hand, not only did not exclude this ultra-sensual region from the scope of their enquiry, but invested it with an importance far above that of the sensual universe. To them knowledge was not confined to what is derived through the agency of the senses alone. They valued it, but they valued the knowledge of the domain within, which lies beyond the world of sense-perception still more. To them, the highest knowledge is that which leads to the salvation of the

Soul. Problems, which engaged their attention most—the great problems of Whence, What, and Whither—are problems which engage the attention of modern scientists the least. In short, Spirit was the sovereign of ancient culture, as Matter is that of modern culture.

This subordination of the animal to the spiritual wants of life made the ancients seek happiness by self-denial rather than by self-indulgence, by curtailing the wants of life rather than by increasing them, by suppressing desires rather than by gratifying them, by lowering the standard of material comfort rather than by raising it. Renunciation was one of the fundamental principles of culture with the Hindus as well as with the Mohamedans. The ascetics irrespective of caste or creed were respected, venerated, nay even worshipped by them and formed an important bond of union between them. "I was very soon attracted" says J. Routledge "by the fact that while wealth nearly always is the chief means of distinguishing man from man in England, it has no such exclusive power in India. There are few sights more pitiable than the dovotee. His whole life is to outside beholders one of misery. But what is he honoured for ? Not wealth ; for he is often wretchedly poor. He is honoured for his presumed piety, for his devotion to the Creator. He has subdued the flesh with its affections and lusts, has brought the body into subjection to the spirit ; has risen above time and lives in eternity." *

The principle of Renunciation by leading to simple living among the people minimised intensity of the struggle for animal existence and inordinate greed and thus promoted concord and amity. But now, under Western influence, God and the Soul are being gradually relegated, as in the West, to the limbo of futilities, one of the basic principles of Western culture being that the well-being of man is to be mainly secured through the outer, rather than the inner man, by multiplying his physical wants, and by inventing means and appliances for gratifying them. The propagation under Western influence in India of this gospel of sensegratification, euphemestically called, "elevation of the standard of living" has proved an almost unmitigated evil. I have shown elsewhere how it has contributed to the impoverishment of the country, and how it has prejudiced health. For our present subject, it is enough to point out that the taste for the infinity of inutilities, superfluities, futilities and fatuities which it has developed, has enormously added to the cost of living, and has, therefore, inordinately increased the stringency of the struggle for existence. One

* "English Rule and Native opinion in India," p. 275,

of the inevitable results of this stringency has been "cut-throat" competition between individuals and classes, and consequent enhancement of greed, selfishness, jealousy and dissension. The cult of "can I kill thee or cans't thou kill me", of "Each for himself and devil take the hindmost" now pervades society. Another pernicious result which has had a disruptive influence upon society is the prevailing tendency of the substitution of the urban for the healthier and more restful rural life. The ties of mutual service and sympathy which bind together the different classes in the village are rudely severed in the town where cashnexus forms the sole bond of connection between them. Hindu Moslem riots are seldom heard of in vIllages. They occur chiefly in cities like Calcutta, Bombay, Delhi, Allahabad, Jubbulpore &c.

2. Hindu-Moslem Pact.

Then, again, one of the outstanding features in which Western civilization differs from the Indian is the immense importance it attaches to politics. Political activities have for some time past over-shadowed all others in the West. Such has also been the case in new India. Its leaders have been seeking to infuse into our people the Western national spirit, and as the principal step thereto striving for unity in the Western sense, which does not necessarily imply amity. In the West, a nation may be split by bitter factional quarrels, but all parties, though they may hate and fight one another, would combine for national aggrandisement, and present a united front to a common enemy. The "nation-builders," as they have been called, of new India, in their anxiety to establish a similar unity, have not only been looking on with complacent equanimity, but have often been taking an active part in the disruption of the forces which held together the heterogeneous communities of old India. No doubt, the Indians can now present a more united front to Government than ever before, as was well seen during the height of the Non-co-operation movement when the prospect of the speedy attainment of Swaraj was held out to them. But the unity being on a purely pragmatic and political basis not only does not connote communal cordiality, but has sometimes been achieved and maintained by measures which are distinctly detrimental to it.

In order to win the support of the Mahomedans, the Indian National Congress in their Lucknow Session entered into a pact with them which recognised the principle of communal representation according to their numerical strength. There was thus secured temporary political unity. But permanent national solidarity was sacrificed, and the breach effected between the two communities by the overthrow of their culture and along with it the pacific traits of character it developed was widened. As the Sanskrit *sloka* has it,—

Na Jātu Kāmas Kāmānūm Upabhogen
Shāmyati
Habishā Krishnavartmeva Bhuyopyabhi-
bardhate.

(Desire is never gratified by its satisfaction, but as in the case of fire fed by clarified butter increases all the more).

The seed sown by the Lucknow pact developed into the pact which the Swarajists of Bengal subsequently entered into in their frantic efforts for the maintenance of Hindu-Moslem political unity. It adumbrates the preposterous principle that not only representation on Legislative bodies and District and Local Boards and Municipalities, but state appointments also should be proportionate to the numerical strength of the different communities,—a principle better calculated to exacerbate intercommunal relations, less conducive to abiding national solidarity, and more prejudicial to the best interests of Swaraj worth having could hardly be conceived.

This was an inevitable result and might have been foreseen but for the inordinate anxiety of Hindu leaders to secure temporary political unity. How hollow is such unity obtained and maintained by pandering to "communal jealousies" is shown, among other things, by the reason assigned by a Mahomedan member of the Bengal Legislative Council, for joining the Swarajya party. "Did not the whole Moslem community", says he "co-operate with the Government long enough? Did not the Moslems of India remain aloof from the Congress and other political agitations from the time of Sir Sayed Ahmed? Have they received their just rights and recognition from Government? It is an open secret, that they have all along been treated as beggars, a race of hewers of wood and drawers of water. The homily of self-help was preached to them in season and out of season by successive Lieutenant Governors.... Did not they side with the Government during the anti-partition agitation? And what was their reward? They were thrown over-board unexpectedly and left at the mercy of the community against which they revolted to please the Government!" This discloses the cloven foot of the political unity of the Swarajya party and shows that the Muslim support of Swaraj is generally not the outcome of the broad-minded farsighted view of the good of the nation as a whole, but of the narrow-minded, short-sighted view of what they consider to be the good of their community.

No doubt with Mahomedan support the Hindu leaders of the Swarajya party, several of whom, I must say, are self-sacrificing patriots of great parts, have secured notable victories over Government. But they are, of a meteoric character, after all, imposing mainly from a spectacular stand-point. They will not deter Government from having its way and from continuing its policy. Besides, the same selfish considerations which have led Mahomedan gentlemen to give their support to the Swarajya party may at any time induce them to withdraw it.

In his presidential address at the Belgaum session of the National Congress, Mahatma Gandhi rightly observed that, "our goal must be removal at the earliest possible moment of communal or sectional representation. A common electorate must impartially elect its representatives on the sole ground of merit. Our services must likewise be manned by the most qualified men and women." But, having to reconcile the divergent interests of the parties he had to lead, he went on to make the significant concession, that "till that comes and communal jealousies or preferences (prejudices) become a thing of the past minorities who suspect the motives of majorities must be allowed to have their way." This concession, no doubt secures temporary political unity but, I am afraid, at the sacrifice of the permanent interests of the nation. When Mahatma Gandhi spoke of "minorities" he had, we take it, our Mahomedan brethern especially in view. To allow them to "have their way" means, we suppose, that they are to continue to have sectional representation on the Councils, and to contend for what they consider to be their right to be represented on the services according to their numerical strength. If they are allowed this gratification is it possible that the goal of the "removal of communal representation" will ever be reached and that "communal jealousies or prejudices" will ever "become a thing of the past"? Are they not likely, rather, to extend and intensify, as is the nature of evil desires, like fire fed by ghee? We do not know of any political or psychological alchemy which by satisfying the base, leaden impulses of human nature can transform them into the golden ones of self-sacrificing duty and genuine patriotism. It is true, satiety occasionally, leads to renunciation. But not generally. It would, for instance, be a very risky thing to allow people who are developing a taste for spirituous liquors to have their way in the hope that they will ultimately give them up and become total abstainers.

That with the experience of the baneful results of the Lucknow pact, a leader of Mahatma Gandhi's calibre should have been compelled to make such a suicidal compromise shows how extremely difficult it is for politicians to properly weigh highly involved and much mixed sociological factors and take long-sighted views in regard to them. The concession which the Hindu leaders of the National Congress at Lucknow made to their Mahomedan colleagues was in regard to representation on the Council. But this was only the thin end of the wedge. Our Mahomedan friends have not been slow to extend the principle underlying the Lucknow pact to District Boards and Municipalities and to services.

3. Communal representation on the Legislative bodies

The illustrious authors of the Montagu Chelmsford Reform scheme proposed to "call forth Indian nationhood." The London *Spectator* observed at the time it was published, that "our Government have an extraordinary aptitude for throwing down apples of discord. ... But the Montagu Report throws down a whole orchard crop." "Divide et impera" has never been the declared policy of our Government. On the contrary, it is professed to be the promotion of concord among the various castes and sects of the Indian community. As a matter of fact, however, measures have been adopted by them which have had the effect not of promoting good feeling, but of sowing dissension, not of strengthening the national bond, but of weakening it.

In justice to the authors of the Montagu scheme, one should say that in respect of Communal representation recommended by them the leaders of the Indian National

Congress showed the way; and the justness of their criticism on the way in which the political union between Hindus and Muslims was achieved in December, 1916, cannot be disputed. The Hindu and Muslim leaders sacrificed permanent to temporary, national to communal interests. The authors are quite justified in thinking, that "so long as the two communities entertain anything like their present views as to the separateness of their interests," they cannot achieve "unity of purpose or community of interest." They strongly condemn communal representation "as a very serious hindrance to the development of the self-governing principle." Yet they suggest that it should be granted to the Muhammadans and the Sikhs. This is like piling faggots on fire while bewailing its destructive effects. The argument they adduce for the step they recommend is very fallacious. "The Muhammadans", they say, "regard separate representations and communal electorates as their only adequate safeguards, But apart from a pledge which we must honour until we are released from it, we are bound to see that the community secures adequate representation in the new councils. How can we say to them that we regard the decision of 1909 as mistaken, that its retention is incompatible with progress towards responsible government, that its reversal will eventually be to their benefit; and that for these reasons we have decided to go back on it?"

The circumstances under which separate electorates were granted to the Muslims in 1909 were quite different from those of 1917. The Morley-Minto Reforms did not contemplate Parliamentary Responsible Government. The Legislative Councils were expanded, to rally the moderate leaders of the National Congress, but their advisory character remained unchanged; and communal representation on advisory councils cannot do much harm, if any. Lord Morley declared emphatically:

"If my existence, either officially or corporeally, were prolonged twenty times longer than either of them is likely to be, Parliamentary system in India is not the goal to which I, for one moment, would aspire."

But the Montagu-Chelmsford scheme professes to lead to Responsible Parliamentary Government; and they themselves show that communal representation would be suicidal to it and to the nationhood they want to call forth. We see no valid reason why they were bound to see that the Muhammadans should secure "adequate representation in the new councils", why they could not tell them that the decision of 1909, if not mistaken, was arrived at under conditions entirely different from the present, that "its retention is incompatible with progress towards responsible government," as they knew full well it is, and "that its reversal will eventually be to their benefit," as they firmly believed it would be. The creation of Communal electorates by the Montagu-Chelmsford Reform scheme has considerably aggravated the tension between Hindus and Moslems caused by the decay of their culture under Western influence.

III

Communal tension between higher and lower castes and between caste Hindus and "Untouchables" caused by present methods of uplift in the material plane.

The tension between the higher and the lower castes among the Hindus, and between the caste Hindus and the "untouchables" is only a degree less acute than that between the Hindus and the Moslems.* Inequality is one of the fundamental laws of nature—inequalities between races, between sexes, between families and between individuals. It became more and more pronounced as society advanced in civilization and complexity. The backward peoples were reduced to the position of "hewers of wood and drawers of water." Even among the superior races, inequalities of physical and intellectual powers gave rise to glaring differ-

* The President at a recent Non-Brahmin Conference at Warda is reported to have said that the Brahmins ought to be eliminated "more especially from Government Services" and characterised them as "plague-rats, wolves and butchers".

ences of social status and to anomalies in the possession of what are popularly called the good things of the world. This inequality has always pressed heavily upon the conscience of sages especially in India where the caste-system has made it to a great extent hereditary. They have, therefore, from the time of Gautama Buddha to that of Ramkrishna Paramhansa, always endeavoured to remove the barriers of caste and minimise its hardships and disabilities.

"Untouchability" in India, originally mainly a hygienic measure, has petrified into an adamantine custom. The reformers of old India like Gautama Buddha, Sankaracharya, Ramananda, Kabir, Nanak, Chaitanya, and Rammohan Roy, who until recently attempted its removal did so without antagonising the different classes, and creating communal conflict. They were all men of high spiritual and ethical development. They were fully cognisant of the supreme value of altruism as the most salient of all the factors that make for the well-being of humanity and as the fountain-head of all virtues, and would not countenance anything which might lead to its attenuation to any serious extent. What they all strove for was equality in the ethical and spiritual plane which promoted amity and concord. The present-day Neo-Indian reformers, on the other hand, obsessed by the Western superstition of equality* adopt methods of uplift which foster dissension and discord where formerly there was good feeling and concord.

"Untouchability" is undoubtedly the worst of the ancient superstitions still prevalent in India. But the modern superstition of equality by the spread of which it is sought to be removed appears to us to be a deal worse. As a consequence of its propagation, our social atmosphere is becoming saturated with bitterness, jealousy, and hatred; class warfare is being waged all over India, the "untouchables" against caste Hindus, and the lower against the higher castes. The worship of the equality fetish having material devolopment and sensual enjoyment as its objective is slowly sapping the foundations of Hindu society by severing the bonds of benevolence and reverence which formerly cemented it.

The "loaves and fishes" of office and seats on Legislative bodies are the principal bones of contention.† Under British rule village self-government having been suppressed, and educational and various other national activi-

* The writer has dealt with this superstition at some length in his work, "Some Present-day Superstitions."

† The "Depressed classes of the Madras Presidency in their Memorandum to the Statutory Commission ask that there should be one member from their Community to the Viceroy's Cabinet, and at least two in each Provincial Cabinet. Fifty per cent. of the officers recruited for the army

ties having been absorbed by the bureaucarcy, multifarious openings have been created in the infinity of services which have sprung up ; and the higher castes who are of Aryan blood, much diluted though it may be in many cases, on account of their intellectual superiority have had a preponderant share of them.* It is much to be doubted whether on the whole they are healthier and happier than the other classes, or whether the work they do is nobler and more beneficent than what is performed by the others. The latter, however, puffed up with false ideas of equality get jealous of the former, especially of the more high-placed among them who (at least the great majority of them), it should be noted, afford some justification for such ill-feeling by casting to the winds the high principle of renunciation (and its concomitant simple living) which characterised their forefathers, and becoming Mammon-worshippers like the Westerners,

---

and navy and a proportionate share in the Civil Services are demanded by them. The subject of the depressed classes should be made a portfolio under the charge of a depressed class member in the Viceroy's Cabinet, and a definite proportion of revenue of the Central and Provincial Governments should be set apart for them.

* According to the Census Report of 1911, in Bengal, Bihar, Orissa and Assam, of 2305 gazetted appointments, about eight-ninths were held by members of the Brahman, Vaidya, and Kayastha castes.

flaunt Western ways of luxurious living before them. The Dravidians and other Non-Aryan races have for three generations enjoyed not only equality of opportunity, the State and State-aided schools and colleges being open to all irrespective of caste or creed, but in many cases some special privileges also. If they have not been able to compete with the other classes, it is because of the inexorable laws of inequality and heredity. Environment can do a great deal to counteract the effects of these laws, but however much it may be made favourable, it is only hare-brained enthusiasts that can expect it to nullify them altogether. From time immemorial, the Indians of Aryan descent have proved themselves to be intellectually superior to those of Non-Aryan descent. Individuals from among the latter may occasionally rival the best endowed scions of the Aryan stock. But they are to be regarded as spurts of Nature like the Negro prodigies of America. The Non-Aryans are fully aware of this, and despairing of ousting the Aryans in open competition, their spokesmen have of late been making the preposterous demand that the Services should be manned in proportion to the numerical strength of the different classes, a demand which despite its apparent absurdity is being countenanced by some of our progressive reformers. The learned professions of Law and Medicine also which, like the Services, have been continually expanding under Western influence attract thousands of our educated young men from the different strata of our society. Owing to this hankering after and rush for service and learned profession, the more promising aud resourceful of our agricultural and trading classes (who alone are able to receive high education) abandon agriculture and trade, which, on account of their hereditary aptitude, they might have improved, and in which they would, at least, have made a secure living, to overcrowd the ranks of penurious *Umedwars* for service, and of impecunious physicians and lawyers. This is more especially the case in Bengal where high English education has made the greatest progress, and the consequent subjugation of indigenous by Western culture has been most complete. The trade of Bengal, which was formerly in the hands of Bengalis, has to a large extent, been captured by trading castes from other parts of India who do not affect such education. The intensity of the struggle for existence among the Bhadralok class which is being constantly recruited from below is thus enormously increased. Their economic condition is every year becoming more and more deplorable, and the unemployment problem among them more and more acute. If there is any really "depressed" class just now, it is they who constitute it, and there is created the paradoxical situation, that large numbers are translated from the so-called "depressed" classes to the middle class only to find themselves more depressed than before. No doubt, a few among them rise to positions which were formerly the preserves of the higher castes ; but the great majority suffer. Struggling for posts the wages of which they have by adding to the keenness of competition brought down to figures which would be derogatory even to artisans and others who have not to maintain the genteel appearance of the Bhadralok class.

Thus the economic result of the "uplift" movement, instead of compensating the heavy ethical loss it has inflicted by propagating the "religion of enmity" at the expense of that of amity, appears to us to have been almost equally disastrous.

That untouchability is an evil is unquestionable, and there can be no two opinions among really enlightened Hindus that it should be removed so far as practicable. Immemorial custom has, however, so firmly ingrained it in the Hindu constitution, that it would be idle to expect its complete removal. All that we can reasonably hope is to mitigate and minimise it. The methods of "uplift" which have of late been in vogue in New India while doing this in a small way, have, as we have seen above, been accompanied by evils of a much more serious character. Reform which instead of adding to that most valuable asset of humanity, benevolence, leads to a serious diminution of it, is a delusion and a snare.

CHAPTER VI

DECAY OF INDIGENOUS INDUSTRY

I

Causes of India's recent industrial decadence: Industrial revolution in Europe.

As we saw in a previous chapter, the industrial independence of India was maintained during the earlier years of British Rule. In fact, her industrial situation then was probably better than that of England. Calicoes had long been exported from India before they could be manufactured in England. English cloth had to be sent to Holland to be bleached or dyed, while dyeing was a flourishing industry in India. The silk-trade of England had to be protected in 1765 by the exclusion of the French silk from English markets. The English were indebted for the finer varieties of linen to Germany and Belgium, while India manufactured muslins of such exquisite fineness, that a piece could be made fifteen yards wide, weighing only 900 grains. England imported nearly two-thirds of the iron and much of the salt, earthenware &c. used by her.

But since the middle of the last century, the economic position of India has undergone a most deplorable change. Her indigenous industrial fabric has been shattered, and she has been reduced from the economically sound position of industrial independence to the very unsound one of industrial servitude, and from that of one of the wealthiest countries of the world to one of its poorest.

One of the most important causes of this industrial decadence was the Industrial Revolution in Europe due to the introduction of labour saving machinery. While Europe was being industrially modernised, India remained in the old-world condition. She was too far from Europe to feel the quickening impulse of progress which transformed that continent; and centuries of slow evolution had given the social structure of the Hindus a rigidity which unfitted it for the ready reception of a sudden impulse. And the marvellous quickness and suddenness of the Industrial Revolution did not give the Indians any time to adapt themselves to the new order of things. English manufactures poured in, like an avalanche, and swept the indigenous industries before them. The day of manual skill, in which the Indian artisans excelled, was over. Hand-made manufactures could no longer compete with machine-made manufactures. Indian artisans had neither the time nor the education to assimilate the mechanical skill of modern Europe. It was not to be expected that illiterate weavers, or illiterate dyers, or illiterate miners would apply the scientific methods of modern industries to their occupations. If

Absence of protective tariff.

India had her own way, she would probably have protected her industries as most civilized countries protect theirs at the present day. But India could not have her own way; a protective tariff by a British Government against British manufactures was not to be thought of.

Thus the first effect of the industrial expansion of England was the ruin of the artisan population of India. The introduction of the power-loom at first caused great distress among the weavers of England also. They invoked the help of Parliament. "They begged to be sent to Canada. They proposed that the terrible power-loom should be restrained by law ; and when that was denied them, they rose in their despair and lawlessly overthrew the machines which were devouring the bread of their children." * But, the distress of the English weavers was only temporary. They soon had a share in the wealth created by the expansion of the cotton industry. It was not till the middle of the nineteenth century that the mechanical skill of modern Europe was transported to India, and the mills and factories on modern methods found employment for a small fraction of the artisans who were thrown out of work by the importation of the English manufactures. But the great majority of the displaced artisans

* "The 19th Century" by R. Mackenzie (1892) P. 72.

have been thrown upon agriculture for subsistence.

The Railways.

Besides the absence of a protective tariff the construction of railways which has been going on apace since the middle of the last century has by facilitating the transport of imported goods proved an important cause of the decadence of indigenous industry. It is true, the railways have developed the export trade in raw produce. But the cultivator, if he gains at all, does not gain to the extent it is generally supposed. The yield from his land has not been sensibly affected by the railways. It is the same now as it was in pre-railway times or even less. He unquestionably gets better prices for his crops. But a portion of the increased profits is consumed in enhanced rent. A portion also goes to pay enhanced wages for labourers, though unfortunately the enhancement is not in the same proportion as that of the prices of food grains. The profits which he has left after meeting these charges may be considered to be the equivalent only of the grain he would have stored, had not the introduction of railways offered him tempting prices to sell it. Whether he is any gainer for having cash instead of a store of grain is a very doubtful point, especially when we consider that the temptation to spend money where one has it in hand, upon festivities and upon various imported articles which the railway has brought to his doors and which mostly partake of the nature of inutilities, futilities and fatuities is very great. The danger of these articles consists in their attractiveness and comparative cheapness. The cultivator and his family probably make a better show of respectability than they ever did before. But when famine threatens they find they have little money and no store of grain to fall back upon. And famines have become more frequent of late than ever before.*

True the railways have facilitated the transport of food to famine stricken districts. But they have also resulted in conditions which are favourable to famines. In the first place, they have by facilitating the transport of imported goods helped to destroy indigenous industries. The artisans whom these industries afforded occupation have been yearly swelling the number of needy peasants and labourers. No doubt some of them have found employment in the railway workshops, and many more find work in the mines, factories and plantations which the railways have helped to develop. But their number is very small, just a little over two millions. Besides, as the largest and most important of the new industries with but few exceptions are owned and

---

* Digby's "Prosperous British India" pp. 130—131.

managed by foreigners, their profits swell the economic drain from India which leads to her impoverishment. The great majority of the displaced artisans have been driven to be labourers or agriculturists. Large towns with urban populations have dwindled into inconsiderable villages. The increase of agricultural at the sacrifice of artisan population is certainly not advantageous for India. There can be no doubt that a great portion of her wealth depended upon her manufacturing industries, as indeed the wealth of every country must do. Down to the early years of the last century she did not export her food grains, but cotton, silk and various other manufactures. It was especially to participate in the trade of these manufactures that the Portuguese, the Dutch, the French and the English came to India.

Then, again, the Railways have contributed to the impoverishment of India as she has long had to remit to England a large amount as interests for them. As has been observed by H. J. S. Cotton, "the country is too poor to pay for its elaborate railway system......and being compelled to borrow in England, has incurred an ever-accumulating debt at what has unfortunately proved to be an ever-increasing rate of interest."* Moreover, what with the obstruction to drainage caused by the embank-

* "New India" p. 61.

ments of railways and their feeder roads in many parts of the country, notably in Bengal, and the pestilential pools choked with weeds on either side of them, they have been the main cause of the fulminant type of malaria which has prevailed since their construction. * The evil effects of Malaria in Bengal are summed up in the Census Report of 1911:

> "Year by year fever is silently at work. Plague slays its thousands, fever its ten thousands. Not only does it diminish the population by death, but it reduces the vitality of the survivors, saps their vigour and fecundity, and either interrupts the even tenour, or hinders the development of commerce and industry. A leading cause of poverty—and of many other disagreeables in a great part of Bengal—is the prevalence of malaria. For a physical explanation of the Bengali lack of energy malaria would count high."

Thus the railway has directly and indirectly contributed to the decay of indigenous industry.

Approximation to the English style of living

The present system of Education on Western lines is to be placed in the same catagory as the railway. It has most dexterously forged links for the ever-lengthening chain of India's industrial bondage. Yet, the press and platform of New India rend the skies with cries for its extension and the expansion of a department which may more appropriately be called nation-destroying than nation-building. As was predicted by Macaulay, it has tended

* "Survival of Hindu Civilization part 2 Physical Degeneration, its causes and Remedies," pp. 21—26.

to approximate our style of living to the English standard. This "elevation" (as it is euphemistically called) is an undoubted fact and is noticeable more or less among nearly all classes of the community especially in the vicinity of of railways. It consists of:—

(1) The substitution of the finer and cheaper mill-made, especially imported, fabrics for the coarser and dearer, though much more substantial and durable hand-made clothes, and the more plentiful use of the former in the form of shirts, coats, etc.; of expensive exotic games for inexpensive indigenous games ; of cigarette for *hooka* smoking ; of imported China glass and enamelled ware for indigenous metallic crockery &c., fine shoes for coarse sandals, sugar for *gur*, bottled and tinned medicines and foods, for indigenous simples and fresh foods ; and of strong liquor for home brewed ale, and its increased consumption.

(2) The acquisition of such habits as tea-drinking and of a taste for expensive musical instruments, such as harmonium, gramophone, etc., and for urban amusements, such as theatres, cinemas, etc.

The quantity of clothing now needed in a household is treble, quadruple or more of what would have been sufficient a generation or two ago. All the members of a middle class family, male and female, infant and adult, must be draped in the various appendages of Western habiliment in conformity with Western fashion as far as possible. Bare legs and bare body would shock the current ideas of decency and æsthetics. The feet must be shod with boots and shoes of Western shape and style which are much more expensive and much less durable than those of indigenous make which were formerly in vogue. Cheap native toys no longer amuse our children. Our young men no longer find pleasure in native games and athletic exercises which cost nothing, but must have football, tennis, badminton, cricket, billiards &c. which cost a great deal. Indigenous entertainments and amusements for which the great majority had to pay nothing have been superseded by theatres, circuses, cinemas &c. which every body must pay for. House-keeping in the old style which utilised the resources of the country to the fullest possible advantage, recognised the tending of the cow as one of its most important duties, and turned out delicacies and artistic utilities out of inexpensive things is a vanishing art in new India. The auditory nerve of the Neo-Indian responds less and less to the notes of indigenons musical instruments, and they are being replaced by the harmonium, and latterly also, to some extent at least, by the gramophone. His tongue is becoming more and more insensible to the taste of Indian dainties, and must have a variety of tinned and bottled foods, solid and liquid. His eyes refuse more and more to be satisfied unless his house is furnished and decorated in the Western fashion, and his grounds laid out with exotic flowers. And his olfactory nerve is becoming more and more obtuse to any fragrance but that of perfumes either genuinely foreign or foreign in native guise. He is giving the go-by to simple indigenous remedies, and apothecary shops whose number in large cities is legion can hardly keep pace with his ailments and are making deplorable inroads into his purse—shops in regard to which an eminent medical authority has declared, that "the world would be better off if the contents were emptied into the sea though the conseqence to the fishes would be lamentable," and that too in the West where the drugs are available in much fresher condition.

This approximation to the European style of living can hardly be called "elevation." In many, I may say most, respects, the change is decidedly for the worse. In a climate where minimum of clothing conformably to the indigenous standard of decency is conducive to health for the greater portion of the year, covering one-self up from head to foot after the European style cannot but be prejudicial to health. The same remark applies generally to the change of taste in regard to eating, drinking and smoking, especially in regard to the alarming spread of tea-drinking and of cigarette smoking.

But whether "elevation" or not, whether for good or for bad, the approximation of the standard of living of one of the poorest communities of the world to that of one of the richest is suicidal. True a very small section of our community composed of some artisans, stateservants, lawyers &c. have more money than before. But they too are generally impoverished.

Impoverishment is a comparative term. If one having comparatively more money than before, has yet less for his wants, he is certainly poorer. I do not think I am exaggerating when I say that the great majority of our middle class have been impoverished in this sense. The candle burns at both ends. Their resources are exhausted on the one hand by the inordinate enhancement of the prices of indigenous necessaries, and on the other by the so called "elevation" of the standard of living which is enlarging their wants. Even incomes which formerly would have been regarded as opulence are now hardly deemed to be bare competence. While milk and the various preparations of milk which form our principal articles of nutrition suited to the climate have become so very dear that the great majority of our middle class cannot afford to get them in sufficient quantity for bare subsistence, they have to spend comparatively large sums upon the gratification of the new tastes which have sprung up for clothing, shoes, socks &c. and for amusements and games, such as theatrical performances, circuses, cinemas, billiards, football, tennis &c. which have superseded the much less expensive indigenous amusements and games. For, the average man blindly follows the prevailing fashion ; and with him show counts for more than substance, and the ornamental prevails over the useful.

The so called "rise" in the standard of living of the people we are talking of has had very far-reaching consequences of a most baneful character. Though frequently descanted upon as an indubitable index of prosperity, it has, in reality, proved a potent cause of the impoverishment not only, directly, of the great majority of the people who affect it, but also, indirectly, of the community as a whole. In the first place it runs away with resources which should be husbanded for improving agriculture and other industries. Secondly, it entails an enormous increase in the consumption of imported articles which accelerates the decadence of indigenous industry and swells the volume of oconomic drain from the country. The writer recently visited a village, among the weaving population of which the Ranchi Co-operative Central Bank (the central organisation for financing Co-operative credit societies in the Ranchi district) had been making a highly praiseworthy attempt to introduce the flyshuttle loom. One of the most serious objections which the weavers urged against the use of this improved loom was, that they could not find a good market even for the scanty produce of the primitive looms which they had been used to ; what are they to do with the increased outturn of the improved looms ? Yet all the male villagers who congregated round us, including even the weavers themselves, were, almost without exception, well habited in mill made clothes ! It is only the females who still affect the coarse and durable wide-bordered *saris.* The special encouragement which is being given to female education will, no doubt, soon do away with even this small amount of patronage which indigenous industry still receives from them. For in towns they too, especially the literates among them, almost universally adopt the current fashion which favours the more showy, but less lasting mill-made fabrics.

The system of elementary education.

A broad survey of the results of the system of elementary education which has been spreading in India for well-nigh three generations has forced the conviction upon us that it has not made the cultivators better cultivators, nor the artisans and tradesmen more efficient artisans and tradesmen than before. On the contrary, it has distinctly diminished their efficiency by inculcating in the literate proletariat a strong distaste for their hereditary mode of living and hereditary callings, and an equally strong taste for brummagem fineries and for occupations of a more or less parasitic nature. They have accelerated rather than retarded the decadence of indigenous industries and have thus helped to aggravate their own economic difficulties and those of the entire community. The following remarks which the Superintendent of the Lushai Hills made sometime ago in regard to the effect of education on the Lushais apply also to the major portion of the mass of the people in other parts of India, especially to the aboriginal section of it—

"They are showing a strong tendency to desert agriculture, their hereditary occupation, and live by their wits. They have undoubtedly more money to spend or waste. This is evidenced by the change which is taking place in their dress. Stout homespun cloths are being discarded for foreign apparel, such as shirts, trousers or "shorts," coats, caps, etc. Imported yarn is displacing the indigenous article in the manufacture of cloths, and cheap and tawdry articles of personal adornment are becoming very common. Though he may have more money to spend, it is impossible to say that the Lushai is now better off than he used to be. In his village he had all he wanted, and lived a simple and happy life. The effect on his moral character has also been far from satisfactory......It is true that a certain number of the Lushais have taken advantage of the openings for improvement so freely provided by Government and profited by them, but, on the whole the results are depressing, and are such as to give grounds for anxiety for the future welfare of the race."

It is very doubtful if the literate peasantry have "more money to spend or waste" than their unlettered brethren. They generally live far beyond their means; and if some of them have more money, it is usually obtained not by the improvement of agriculture or manufacture, but by occupations of an unproductive, and not unoften also of a shady character, the aspiration of the literate proletariat being to enter some service or live upon their wits. The best patrons of native manufactures are still the illiterate peasantry who have not yet taken to shoddy apparel and "cheap and tawdry articles of personal adornment," at least to the extent the literates have. In fact, it is they, especially their women, who have arrested the utter annihilation of indigenous industry.

The subjects which the current system of education comprises have mostly no immediate reference to the requirements of our cultivators, artisans and traders. Their boys cannot derive any earthly benefit, so far as their hereditary occupations are concerned by memorising the feats of glorified swindlers, thieves and murderers, or by learning the names of mountains, rivers and towns only to be forgotten soon after. If they are sent to schools it is with the view that they may enter some service, preferably Government service, or some profession, preferably the legal profession. The Primary standard is looked upon as a stepping stone to the Middle English or the High School standard, and the High School standard to the Collegiate standard. This is applauded as the "uplift" of the "lower" classes by Government as well as by new India, though it is hardly consonant with common sense to dub the people who pursue agriculture, among whom are to be found representatives of the highest Hindu castes, as "lower" than those who earn their livelihood by service or by some profession of a more or less parasitic character and to regard the translation of the former, into the fold of the latter as uplift. For a generation or so, in tracts which are called backward, that is, where the present system of education has not made much progress as yet, the literates through the favour and patronage of Government and of missionaries, in the case especially of the aboriginal tribes, appear to prosper, and their prospect seems very alluring. But sooner or later they are sure to be threatened with an economic crisis such as the gentry of Bengal are confronted with today.

What our people want is more or better food, and new India vies with the Government in giving them a system of socalled "education" which not only does not enable them to get it, or holds out any reasonable prospect of their ever being able to get it, but, on the contrary, fosters in them tastes and habits which make them despise indigenous products and render them fit subjects for the exploitation of scheming capitalists mostly foreign ; a system which instead of enlightening their intellect so that they may have a proper understanding of their own interests and those of the entire community, obfuscates it so as to make them oblivious of those interests and sacrifice substance to shadow exchanging a good portion of what food they grow, which if kept in the country would make famine a rare* occurrence for imported manufactures a good portion of which might be easily dispensed with, often without any harm and sometimes with considerable advantage ; a system which instead of strengthening their moral fibre weakens it, instead of inculcating in them self-reliance, and the dignity of honest, productive labour makes them averse to it, not unoften of a degrading character, instead of fostering economy and self-control fosters self-indulgence and extravagance. If there is a panacea for our mundane ills, it is wisdom ; and education which does not contribute to its growth is a misnomer.

* The food grains that are exported are usually supposed to represent the surplus left after meeting the requirements of the country. As was observed, however, by Sir William Hunter, if the whole population ate as they should, no such surplus would exist.

III

The indications of impoverishment of the mass of the people under British Rule are unmistakable and are very widespread and general. It has been recognised from its very commencement.

Economic drain due to foreign commercial exploitation, a main cause of Indian's impoverishment.

As long ago as 1790 Lord Cornwallis spoke of "the great diminution of the current specie," and of the "languor which has thereby been thrown upon the cultivation and the general commerce of the country." Later on Mr. Frederick John Shore of the Bengal Civil Service declared more emphatically that "the English Government has effected the impoverishment of the people and country to an extent almost unparalleled," and Bishop Heber wrote that "the country is in a gradual state of impoverishment. The Collectors do not make this avowal officially. ....In general, all gloomy pictures are avoided by them as reflecting on themselves and as drawing on them censure from the Secretaries at Madras or Calcultta." It may be stated, parenthetically, how true *mutatis mutandis* this statement is even at the present day.

The main cause of the impoverishment, the economic drain from India, has also been well recognised from the very beginning of British Rule. Mr. Montgomery Martin writing as early as 1838 when the drain was considerably less than what it is now says :—

> "The annual drain of £3,000,000 on British India has amountedi n thirty years at 12 percent (the usual Indian rate) compound interest to the enormous sum of £723,900,000 sterling! So constant and accumulating a drain, even in England, would soon impoverish her. How severe then must be its effects on India where the wage of a labourer is from two pence to three pence a day."

Mr. Saville Marriot, who was for sometime one of the Commissioners of Revenue in the Deccan, and afterwards a member of Council says speaking of the drain about 1845 when it was considerably less than it is now : "It will be difficult to satisfy the mind that any country could bear such a drain upon its resources without sustaining any serious injury. And the writer [Mr. Marriot] entertains the fullest conviction that investigation would effectually establish the truth of the proposition as applicable to India. He has himself most painfully witnessed it in those parts of the country with which he was connected, and he has every reason to believe, that the same evil exists, with but slight modification, throughout our eastern empire." Again: "Most of the evils of our rule in India arise directly from, or may be traced to the heavy tribute which that country pays to England."

Sir George Wingate who had acquired distinction in the land revenue settlements of the Bombay Presidency wrote about the middle of the last century :—

"With reference to its economical effects upon the condition of India, the tribute paid to Great Britain is by far the most objectionable feature in our existing policy. Taxes spent in the country from which they are raised are totally different in their effects from taxes raised in one country and spent in another. In the former case the taxes collected from the population at large are paid away to the portion of the population engaged in the service of the Government through whose expenditure they are again returned to the industrious classes. They occasion a different distribution, but no loss of national income; and hence it is that in countries advanced in civilization...... an enormous taxation may be realised with singularly little pressure upon the community. But the case is wholly different when the taxes are not spent in the country from which they are raised. In this case they constitute no mere transfer of a portion of the national income from one set of citizens to another, but an absolute loss and extinction of the whole amount withdrawn from the taxed country. As regards its effects on national production, the whole amount might as well be thrown into the sea as transferred to another country, for no portion of it will return from the latter to the taxed country in any shape whatsoever. Such is the nature of the tribute we have so long exacted from India.

"The Indian tribute, whether weighed in the scales of justice or viewed in the light of our true interest, will be found to be at variance with humanity, with common sense, and with the received maxims of economical science." *

"It must be remembered" says Sir G. Campbell "that we give neither our services nor our capital for nothing. Much of this is paid for by remittances to Europe. The public remittances are now £16,000,000 per annum, and it is estimated that the private remittances would be almost as much more if the flow of British Capital to India were stopped and the transactions showed only sums received in England. As it is, the continual addition of fresh capital invested in India about balances. The private remittances, and the balance of trade show only about the same amount as the public drawings to be depleted from India—that is about £16,900,000 per annum. This is what is sometimes called "Tribute" paid to England. Well, it is not tribute, but it is paid for civil and military services, loans, railways, industrial investments, and all the rest ; and the result is that a large part of the increased production is not retained by the Indian peasant." †

The economic drain from India is two-fold due partly to political and partly to industrial and commercial causes. The Home Charges constitute the bulk of the former and have increased considerably since the beginning of the last century. In 1834-35, the amount did not exceed three millions, but in 1911-12, it was nearly nineteen millions sterling. However regrettably high the Home Charges may be, a sober consideration of the various items composing them would lead one to the conclusion

* "Our Financial Relations with India," pp. 56-64.

† "The British Empire" p. 70

that they are not reducible to any very considerable extent even with the problematical grant of the "Responsible Government" which has been promised in some form or other.

Resuscitation of indigenous industry by the positive method not hopeful.

The solution of the problem of the impoverishment of India thus depends mainly upon the reduction of the drain due to foreign industrial and commercial exploitation. This could be effected in two ways, of which one may be called the positive, and the other the negative. The former consists in the industrial regeneration of India on modern methods by indigenous agency, and the latter in stemming the tide of Western Civilization so as to reduce the imports of foreign manufactures.

In regard to the Positive Method, I must say, I was for a long time partial to it. In the early eighties of the last century I published articles and pamphlets advocating the spread of scientific and technical education and the establishment or expansion of large industries on mdern methods by Indian agency, and there was hardly any Indian Joint Stock Company started at the time in Bengal to which I did not subscribe as my means permitted. Gradually, however, as the evils of Western industrialism grew in extent and enormity, my predilection for modern industry became attenuated. And in 1901 I contributed an article in the "Westminister Review" strongly condemning it. But as a measure of self-defence against foreign commercial exploitation I continued my humble efforts for industrial development on modern methods by indigenous agency in India. Latterly however my enthusiasm for it has suffered considerable abatement. It has been tried during the last four decades, but has on the whole failed; and the following considerations make me pessimistic about its success in the future, at least, to any large extent.

First. Want of capital. The more gigantic the operations, and the more extensive the employment of up-to-date machinery or, in other words, the larger the capital, the more assured will be the success of an industry under modern conditions. We can hardly realise without straining our imagination the titanic industrial investments of the West, and how vast and how very deep is the economic gulf between India and the West. A high authority estimated the hoarded wealth of India sometime ago at three hundred millions sterling. Assuming this estimate to be correct and assuming the whole of it to be available for industrial investments, it would still be less than a sixth of the amount invested in manufacturing industries alone in a single country of the West, the United States of America.* So immense is the economic dispa-

* The capital employed in the manufacturing industries

rity between India and the nations who exploit her, that there appears to me but little chance of her ever being able to compete with them successfully in the sphere of modern industry.

Secondly, India can never expect to adopt the methods of spoliation which have added to the wealth of her industrial rivals. The wealth which poured into England from India between the date of Plassey and that of Waterloo—variously estimated at £500,000,000 to £1,000,000,000—is surmised by some to have been an important, if not the most important factor in the development of her mammoth industries during their infant stages. The industrial revolution of Germany began shortly after the Franco-Prussian War, and it appears to have derived its initial impulse, though indirectly, from the huge indemnity which Prussia wrung from France. The acquisition of Formosa, of the Southern half of Saghalin and of Korea, and the political influence which she established in Manchuria gave immense impetus to the industrial development of Japan.

Thirdly. The political condition of India is such that her Government can do but little to help the development of indigenous enterprises even if it be actuated by a sincere desire to do so.

---

of the United States in 1900, was in round figures £2, 000, 000, 000,

As has been rightly observed by H. J. S. Cotton, "in the great industrial conflict of the world England is engaged in a life struggle against American and Continental competition, and against competition also with her colonies, and our own capitalists are keenly conscious of the fact that they are more and more dependent on their success in exploiting the vast population and natural resources of India to their own benefit. The Government of Lord Curzon has identified itself with this policy; and whatever may be possible in other directions of fiscal enterprise this at least is certain, that having regard to the economic revolution through which India has passed, no attempt can be made to encourage Indian industries, or the investment of Indian capital by means of protective legislation without a complete reversal of British policy, and the sacrifice of the profits and aspirations of British capitalists."

Fourthly. The ethical ideals of the Indians are adverse to industrial development on a large scale as they discourage greed and dissociate industry (except agriculture) from culture. It is true, these ideals are being superseded by Western ideals of material progress, but they still influence large sections of our community to a great extent, and thus the chief motive impulse which impels people to acquire wealth has much less force in India than in the West.

Fifthly. Weak development of industrial qualities. The physical environment of the great industrial powers of the West has made them as eminently active and combative, as that of the Indians has made them inactive (in the Western sense) and pacific. The latter have far more of the gentle qualities developed by a spiritual and quietistic disposition, but far less of the industrial and militant qualities of the former.

Sixthly. The lateness of the industrial movement in India. If it had commenced even five decades ago there would have been a greater chance of success. Within that time, the Westerners and the Japanese have gone so far ahead of us industrially, and have so firmly established themselves in the markets of India that it has been yearly becoming more and more difficult for our countrymen to compete with them. This difficulty is considerably enhanced by the fact that the Young Indians who receive technical education do not enjoy the opportunities which the Westerners have of completing it by practical training in large works.

Thus we find, that the Negative Method is likely to prove of greater importance than the positive in arresting the decay of indigenous industry. But the propagation of the ideas of comfort, decency and æsthetics of Western civilization due to our cultural subjugation makes its adoption extremely difficult. The Neo-Indian is generally so obsessed by the Western idea of decency, that in a climate where airbath is exceedingly pleasant and beneficial to health, he covers himself up *cap-a-pie* so as to stop all passage for the ingress of air. In three decades, between 1881 and 1911 the population of India (including Native States) increased from 258,891,900 to 315,156,396, that is about 21 per cent. Within that time, however, the imports of apparel and of other cotton and woollen manufactures rose in value from Rs. 23,17,10,610 to Rs. 45,62,27,999, that is to say about 96 per cent, and that too while the number of cotton mills in India rose from 58 to 254 and that of woollen mills from 2 to 5. Yet it cannot be said, that two or three generations ago our people were less healthy, less comfortable, and more lacking in the essentials of civilised society than their congeners to day, though the latter present a much smarter appearance so far as habiliments and other externals of civilization are concerned. From my own experience, I can say the former were healthier and happier.

Clothing is the chief item. But there are numberless other items, such as boots and shoes, cigarettes, soaps, liquors, motor cars, sugar, glass and glassware, drugs etc. which usually partake more or less of the character of superfluities, inutilities and futilities. These swell the economic drain from India and further the decadence of indigenous industry. The Swadeshi movement which has been going on during the last two decades appears to have made but little impression upon the imports of manufactures, The truth is for scores, who are strongminded enough to act in conformity with Swadeshi principles, there are thousands who follow the prevailing Western fashion which is being disseminated by railways and state and state-aided sohools and colleges. Yet there is hardly any sign of the abatement of the enthusiasm of New India for their expansion. It is but natural that a British Government should do all it can to secure customers for British manufactures. But it is sheer folly on our part to join hands with them in their endeavour to do so. True, Government dug the ditch in which we are being drowned, but we cannot absolve ourselves from the responsibility of deepening it.

CHAPTER VII.

IS IMITATION POLITICAL SWARAJ DESIRABLE ?

I

Our choice in this world generally lies between evils, and in answering this question we have to discuss whether, under existing conditions, Swaraj on the Western model with Dominion Status (or Imitation Swaraj as it may be briefly called) which the majority of political India at present aspire to, or British Rule is likely to be the lesser evil. The principal charges brought against the latter are:

(1) Economic drain.

(2) Highly expensive administrative machinery.

(3) Repression.

Economic drain not likely to be appreciably reduced under Imitation Swaraj.

The present economic drain from India, as we saw in the last chapter, is two-fold, political and commercial. With the realisation of Swaraj, the Indianisation of the services may be expected to proceed more rapidly than at present, and thus the "Home Charges" on account of pensions, gratuities and furlough allowances may be reduced. But they constitute considerably less than half of the "Home Charges." The interest on debt forms the great bulk, and whether the debt was fair or unfair, it could not be repudiated if India is to remain a partner of the British Empire as the great majority of political India desire she should. So the saving would not be much. Then, again, if the present rage for the Western mode of living continues—and there is no indication of its abatement except in the case of a few individuals—the reduction of drain on account of pensions etc. may be outweighed by an increase in the volume of drain due to commercial exploitation which is far more serious than the drain due to "Home Charges." As we saw in the last chapter, the extension of the socalled "education" of the present day is one of the main causes of the former. In fact, there is no agency which more ingeniously and dexterously forges fetters for our economic bondage, yet the cry for free and compulsory education in New India yearly becomes louder and more insistent. As has been observed by Sir John Woodroffe "were it not that there has been no general primary education, and that such education as is now given is necessarily confined to comparatively few, and to the fact that there has been a rise of national consciousness, the whole of India was likely to have been Anglicised. All this is part of the process whereby a dominant race at first works by force of arms, and then when free to do so by cultural assimilation."*

* "Is India civilized ?" P. 42

Rise of real national consciousness which would free us from the fetters of our cultural subjugation is as yet confined to a small fraction of the Neo-Indian community. Such consciousness in the case of the great majority is chiefly evidenced in occassionally combining to fight the Government. But, as we have seen before, the combination is effected by pacts and other measures which have fostered communal conflict and disintegrated the nation. * Never before were intercommunal and interprovincial jealousy and dissension more rife than at present. Hallelujahs of unity and patriotism are punctuated by jeremiads on communal discord. An occasional unselfiesh patriotic cry of "Swaraj for India" is drowned among a multiplicity of selfish unpatriotic cries of "Swaraj for Islam", "Swaraj for the low castes and untouchables", "Swaraj for peasants and labourers," "Behar for the Beharees", "Assam for the Assamese" etc. We are strongly inclined to think that the good resulting from fights with Government is greatly outweighed by the evil resulting from fights among the different groups into which the nation has been divided.

The two methods by which the volume of the present colossal drain due to commercial exploitation could be diminished are the same

---

* Vide *ante* chapter V

as those by which as we have seen in the last chapter, indigenous industry could be regenerated—the Positive and the Negative. The former has hitherto not met with any large measure of success and we are pessimistic about its future.* We have, therefore, to depend chiefly upon the Negative method, which would necessitate our going back to the simple living that obtained two or three generations ago. This presupposes the superiority of Indian to present day Western culture, which is not only not admitted by the great majority in political India, but they consider the latter to be far superior to the former. In fact there has recently risen a party of young men who would scrap Indian culture altogether.

It should be noted that the clamant demand for compulsory or free "education" in New India is against the advice of the most thoughtful men of the West who, however, have as little influence there as Indian Sages have in New India. The object of rational education should be moral as well as intellectual development, the former to a greater extent than the latter. But as Herbert Spencer says :—

"So far, indeed. from proving that morality is increased by education, the facts prove, if anything, the reverse.........It has been shown from Government returns "that the number of juvenile offenders in the Metropolis area has been steadily increasing every year since the institution of the Ragged

* Vide *ante* chapter, VI.

School Union, and that whereas the number of criminals who *cannot* read and write has decreased from 24,856 (in 1844) to 22,968 (in 1848), or no less than 1888 in that period the number of those who *can* read and write imperfectly has increased from 33,337 to 36,229, or 2,892 in the same time. Aonther contributor to the series of articles on "Labour and the Poor" from which the above statement is quoted remarks 'that the mining population (in the North) are exceedingly low in point of education and intelligence; and yet they contradict the theories generally entertained upon the connexion of ignorance with crime by presenting the least criminal section of the population of England.' And speaking of the women employed in the ironworks and collieries throughout South Wales he says—'their ignorance is absolutely awful; yet the returns show in them a singular immunity from crime'.........The fact is, that scarcely any connexion exists between morality and the discipline of ordinary teaching. Mere culture of the intellect (and education usually conducted amounts to little more) is hardly at all operative upon conduct.........Intellect is not a power but an instrument—not a thing which itself moves and works but a thing which is moved and worked by forces behind it. To say that men are ruled by reason is as irrational, as to say that men are ruled by their eyes. Reason is an eye—the eye through which desires see their way to gratification. And educating it only makes it a better eye, —gives it a vision more accurate and more comprehensive—does not at all alter the desires subserved by it........... Probably some will urge that enlightening men enables them to discern the penalties which naturally attach to wrong-doing, and in a certain sense it is true. But is only superficially true. Though they may learn that the grosser crimes commonly bring retribution in one shape or another they will not learn that the subtler ones do. Their sins will merely be made more Machiavellian.........Did much knowledge and piercing intelligence suffice to make men good, then Bacon should have been honest, and Napoleon should have been just..........It is, indeed, strange that with the facts of daily life before them in the street, in the counting house, and the family, thinking men should still expect education to cure crime." *

Frederick Harrison said, in an interview published in the *Times* sometime ago that "the boom in education has not brought any nobler literature, any greater art, any purer drama, any finer manners. Serious literature is being choked out by the increased cost of printing, the abolition of a leisured class able to study in peaee and to produce from its learning, and by the mad whirl of modern existence. The result of this chaos in spiritual and moral training is a manifest loosening of the canons of moral life, the defiance of discipline by the young and ambitious, the mockery of age and all the lessons of age ; worst of all, the sacrifice of family as a moral institution, and the degradation of marriage to be a temporary partnership entered into as a frivolous mode of getting 'a good time' and to be cast off as easily as a lodging which is not convenient." The effect of "education" upon the proletariat has been tersely described by John Stuart Mill as only a craving for "higher wages and less work for the sake of more sensual indulgence."

"The lawlessness of our lads" observes general Booth, "the increased license of our girls, the general shiftlessness from the home making point of view of the products of our factories and schools are far from re-assuring. Our young people have never learnt to obey. The fighting gangs of half-grown lads in Lisson Grove, and the scuttlers of Manchester are ugly symptoms of a social condition that will not grow better by being left alone. It is the home that has been destroyed, and with home the homelike virtues. It is the dis-homed multitude, nomadic, hungry that is rearing an undisciplined, population, cursed from birth with

* "Social Statics" (National Education).

hereditary weakness of body and hereditary faults of character." *

Dr. Albert Wilson says in his "Child of Circumstance": "He (the child) is driven into a miscalled education department, and crammed with facts difficult to remember and of no use in after-life."

"I do not care," declares Ruskin emphatically, "that children as a rule should learn either reading or writing, because there are very few people in this world who get any good by either. Broadly and practically, whatever foolish people read does them harm; and whatever they write does other people harm." "Even as appliances to intellectual culture" says Herbert Spencer, "books are greatly over-estimated. Instead of second-hand knowledge being regarded as of less value than first-hand knowledge, and as a knowledge to be sought only where first-hand knowledge cannot be had, it is actually regarded as of greater value. Something gathered from printed pages is supposed to enter into a course of education; but if gathered by observation of Life and Nature, is supposed not thus to enter. Reading is seeing by proxy—is learning indirectly through another man's faculties instead of directly through one's own faculties, and such is the prevailing bias that the indirect learning is thought preferable to the direct learning, and usurps the name of cultivation! We smile when told that savages consider writing as a kind of magic......Yet the current notions about printed information betray a kindred delusion. ......And this delusion, injurious in its effects even on intellectual culture, produces effects still more injurious on moral culture, by generating the assumption that this, too, can be got by reading and the repeating of lessons." "Books are good enough in their way," says Stevenson, "but they are a mighty bloodless substitute for life."

---

* "In Darkest England and the Way out" p. 66.

Despite the warnings of Sages, the politicals of England inaugurated compulsory education as they wanted to "educate their masters." New India has zealously echoed the cry for such education not only for political purposes but also as a principal means of ameliorating the condition of the people. In fact, new India is under the illusion that it will prove to be the panacea for all the evils India is suffering from. "The deathrate," says a Neo-Indian writer, "is increasing alarmingly in the towns through overcrowding, and in the villages through malaria, plague, and contamination of drinking water. Universal education is the only remedy for the evil."* The late Mr. G. K. Gokhale, who devoted his life to the good of his country in a spirit of self-sacrifice unsurpassed in new India, declared : "I am glad there are signs visible on all sides which go to show that this great truth—this profound truth—that there can be no real national progress for our people without universal mass education—this great fundamental and profound truth is being realised in an ampler and ampler measure on all sides of us........That ninety per cent of our people should be sunk in ignorance, superstition and squalor—I can think of no injustice more cruel or monstrous than this."

---

* J. N. Sircar, "Economics of British India" p. xi.

Illiteracy should not be confounded with ignorance, and though our people are poorer there is less of "squalor" among them than among the corresponding classes of the West. Nevertheless, it is highly desirable that literacy of the right sort should spread among the masses. But what with the disproportionately high cost of inspection, the regulation buildings, the regulation furniture, the cost of stationery and text-books (which are often either useless or mischievous) etc. even primary education such as is imparted by the Education Department has become too expensive for the mass of our people. Under existing conditions it is only the well-to-do and the more aspiring among the "lower" classes who are able to send their boys to schools ; and the intelligence, ambition and resources which might have improved agriculture and arrested the decadence of indigenous industry are diverted into courses that lead to the professions and services which are more or less of a parasitic nature. This is a heavy loss. But this is not all. The so-called "education" co-operates with the other forces which such a highly material civilization as the Western has introduced to diffuse among the students a taste for luxuries (in the Indian sense) and inculcate among them Western, ideas of decency, cleanliness and comfort which as we have seen before contribute so conspicuously to swell the economic drain from India.

The Government makes large grants for school buildings and boarding houses and their equipment. In fact, a good percentage of the total grants for education is employed for such purposes. Boys who have been accustomed to live in houses, which to the Westerners appear no better than hovels, and who have always been accustomed to squatting on mats are accommodated in well appointed houses which even the great majority of the middle class gentry can never aspire to live in. Not unoften, they are provided with chairs, benches, almirahs tables, desks, etc. The inexpensive outdoor games which formerly used to amuse and invigorate them have been superseded by much more expensive football, cricket etc. No wonder that under these conditions the sons of strong, sturdy, simple husbandmen should be gradually converted into effeminate, fashionably draped Bhadroloks, and that they should imbibe a distaste for the ungentlemanly occupations of their forefathers. No wonder that such occupations should cease to gratify their enlarged wants and minister to their "civilized" tastes. They undoubtedly assume a showy exterior which to the Western or the Westernised eye is an indubitable index of progress and prosperity of the community, though, in reality it is an index of just the reverse. They carry the torch of "civilization" into their village homes. The fashion set by them is extensively imitated, and thus the "rise" in the standard of living which New India rejoices in spreads far and wide, accelerating the decadence of indigenous industry and swelling the volume of economic drain from the country.

The Registrar of the Co-operative Societies, for Bengal observed sometime ago, that the education which is imparted to the peasantry in the village schools "instead of developing character stunts their moral sense, and encourages a tendency to live more on wits than on manual labour, and easily converts men who would otherwise have been honest into pettifogging touts." "The present system of elementary education I am afraid," says Mr. Abdul Karim, retired Inspector of schools, "has proved a failure as far as the masses are concerned. It has been in operation for a long time, but it has not improved either the knowledge or the condition of the villagers." *

* "In the course of my tours," says Mr. Karim, "while visiting a school in the district of Backerganj I found it would die for want of funds and pupils. I asked the leading people of the locality to meet me at my green-boat after the inspection was over. While I was urging upon them the necessity of maintaining the school by contributing to its funds and by admitting their boys into it, I heard a man whispering that he would give "*Hari Loot*' (A Hindu thanks-giving ceremony) on the day the school would be abolished. When the people were gone, I enquired of the local Inspector of Police, who came to see me why the

There are no doubt individuals in New India who fully recognise the pernicious character of the current system of education. Mahatma Gandhi is reported to have said in an interview

---

residents of the place were disgusted with the school. What he said convinced me that the people had reason to be dissatisfied. The place was largely inhabited by petty shop keepers, who required the assistance of their boys in selling goods and in keeping accounts. But no sooner were the boys admitted into the school than they gave themselves airs and looked down upon shopkeeping as unworthy of the people who could read and write. From what I learnt at this and subsequent inquiries, I have reason to think that the existence of a school in their neighbourhood has been a source of much trouble to many a peasant family. Even against his wish a peasant has to send his boy to the neighbouring school either through the persuasion of the Guru, or on account of the importunity of the boy who wants to join the other boys of the village at school. As soon as the boy enters the school he becomes a different creature. He changes his manners, habits, tastes and even his name. In going through Patshala records it is sometimes found that a boy a part of whose name in the register of the last class was Mandal has changed it in the register of the next class into Bishash, a term which is supposed to signify some literary attainments. His parents not only lose his assistance in tending cattle and cultivating fields, but are also obliged to supply him with good clothes, an umbrella, besides books and writing materials at a cost far beyond their means. After acquiring a smattering of Bengali...........he becomes a burden upon his family and not infrequently a curse to society. For, he creates factions, fosters litigation, and sometimes even teaches perjury and forgery." ("Some Political, Economical and Educational Questions" pp. 5-6)

with the late Motilal Ghosh, that "so long as our boys who are the makers of the future of the country, continue to be intellectually fed in the present day schools there is little hope for the country." "One of the most remarkable features of British Rule in India" says Dr. A.K. Coomarswamy, "has been the fact that the greatest injuries done to the people of India have taken the outward from of blessings. Of this education is a striking example." As we shall see hereafter, earnest attempts are being made in New India to start educational institutions on Indian lines. But the most numerous, the most influential and the most articulate section of the Neo-Indian community still favour the current system of education. It has, for some years past, been, under the Montagu-Chelmsford Reform scheme, what is called a "transferred" subject, that is a subject in charge of Indian Ministers. But neither they nor the Legislative Councils who are supposed to control it have ever made any attempt to change its character. On the contrary, they have always complained of the dearth of funds which stands in the way of its expansion. This shows that the educational policy of the Swaraj government is not likely to be markedly different from what it is at present.

Then, again, its evil effects are being enhanced by the persistent preaching to the proletariat about the necessity of a rise in the standard of living by an increasingly influential socialistic or communistic section of political India. As a consequence, the workers in mills and mines strike for higher wages which as, in the West, means greater sensual indulgence leading to increased consumption of brummagem fineries.

Such 'elevation' no doubt translates the sparsely clad simple rustic into something of a fairly well draped 'gentleman' with 'gentlemanly' tastes,—a transformation which is usually applauded as 'progress.' It undoubtedly benefits the capitalists (mostly foreign) whose object is to exploit the peoples, particularly of Asia and Africa. But does it benefit the latter? Do they become healthier and happier? Decidedly not. The mill hands of Bombay, who, some time back, were described by the *Times of India* as 'Bombay's slaves,' and who are what the protagonists of communism would like the factory and mine labourers of other parts of India to be, are certainly from all accounts much more miserable than any section of their congeners out in the country.

It would probably be urged that 'Bombay's slaves' are no worse than similar workmen in England, and that, in the interests of the community, it may be desirable to sacrifice the happiness and crush the manhood of a section of it. Certainly, from the strictly material standpoint, the formation of an industrial class in the modern sense has added very largely to the wealth and material prosperity of England. But would the creation of a similar class in India add appreciably to her wealth ? I think not and for the following reasons:

First, most of the large industries in India (including Burma) are owned and managed by Europeans, and I have already shown, that, under present conditions, they would always remain overwhelmingly non-Indian. So their profits would mainly go out of the country and the high emoluments of management would be chiefly shared by non-Indians.

Secondly, India, unlike England, is mainly agricultural and will always remain so. Agriculture being the main source of the wealth of the country, anything which interferes with its development is much to be deplored. At present the people who work in industrial concerns may, and sometimes do, on their return to their homes devote a portion of their savings to such development. But that would not be the case if they were enticed away from land altogether by high wages and urban comforts. The propagandists of uplift and of so called 'education' have succeeded in manufacturing a good number of the most resourceful and intelligent of our cultivating class into penurious clerks. The success of the propagandists of industrialism and communism would convert a considerable section of them into slavish adjuncts of the industrial machinery.

As I am writing this, political India is about to launch on a vigorous movement for the boycott of foreign merchandise such as was attempted during the partition agitation in Bengal between 1906 and 1910, and also during the Non-cooperation movement a decade later. The following figures will show how it failed then, and there is hardly any reasonable ground for expecting any greater success now:

Failure of Boycott of Foreign manufactures.

Imports of Merchandise

Rupees.

1905-06—112, 11, 37, 419
1906-07—117, 29, 59, 803
1907-08—136, 64, 75, 561
1908-09—128, 78, 68, 787
1909-10—122, 65, 12, 673
1910-11—133, 70, 57, 458
1911-12—144, 05, 54, 383
1912-13—166, 62, 96, 807
1913-14—191, 30, 79, 586
1914-15—182, 24, 75, 000
1915-16—131, 34, 00, 000
1917-18—150, 42, 51, 000
1918-19—169, 03, 41, 000

Imports of Merchandise

Rupees.

1919-20—207, 97, 24, 000
1920-21—335, 50, 85, 000
1921-22—266, 34, 63, 000
1922-23—232, 70, 77, 000
1923-24—227, 61, 23, 000
1924-25—246, 62, 54, 000
1925-26—226, 17, 78, 000
1926-27—231, 31, 52, 000.

The imports of cotton manufactures (the chief objective of the Boycott movement) during the same period were—

Rupees.

1905-06—42, 50, 80, 556
1906-07—41, 01, 19, 277
1907-08—48, 10, 56, 491
1908-09—38, 07, 77, 023
1909-10—39, 42, 68, 344
1910-11—44, 88, 54, 363
1911-12—49, 63, 28, 832
1912-13—60, 86, 38, 587
1913-14—66, 61, 59, 560
1914-15—48, 54, 90, 000
1915-16—43, 27, 50, 000
1917-18—56, 51, 68, 000
1918-19—60, 55, 48, 000
1919-20—59, 07, 93, 000
1920-21—102,12, 00, 000

Imports of Cotton Manufactures

	Rupees.
1921-22—	56, 93, 81, 000
1922-23—	70, 13, 02, 000
1923-24—	67, 48, 46, 000
1924-25—	82, 32, 51, 000
1925-26—	65, 66, 73, 000
1926-27—	65, 04, 74, 000

II

Expensive character of administration unsuited to the material condition of our people.

The condition of the mass of our people, despite some delusive signs of meretricious prosperity is extremely unsatisfactory, and what is a matter of grave apprehension, has been going from bad to worse. Famines have been becoming more and more frequent, the indebtedness of the peasantry* has gradually assumed such colossal dimensions that there are experienced men who despair of that excellent movement for the establishment of Co-operative Credit Societies ever being able to cope with it; the number and virulence of various diseases, several of which were almost unknown before, have been increasing, and

* Mr. S. S. Thorburn who made a special study of the condition of the peasantry in the Punjab, says that "there was no general indebtedness in any village before 1871". But about two decades later, of 474 villages examined by him he found only 138 slightly involved. Of the remainder he found 210 seriously and 126 hopelessly indebted.

numerous localities once noted for their salubrity are being converted into hot-beds of fever or plague. The fact is, the vitality of our people is diminishing.

"The increasing number of famines and the terrible mortality which results from them," says Sir H. J. S. Cotton, "in spite of all the exertions of the Government and the heroic efforts of individual officers, are—if there were no other evidence—an overwhelming demonstration that the capacity of the people to maintain themselves in on the decline......... The reason why famines are more frequent than formerly and more severe, is that the resources of the people are less able to resist them."

The Government are, I believe, aware, at least partly, of this deplorable state, and, I have not the shadow of a doubt, are anxious to remedy it. But their remedy consists chiefly in multiplying or amplifying their departments. Administration has been gradually becoming more and more top-heavy. In fact, the regulative and social structure of India has been gradually assuming the form of an inverted pyramid, with a very small but well-to-do class of State officials, lawyers, money-lenders etc. at the top, a discontented impecunious middle class lower down, and an impoverished peasantry at the base. Unless further progress of such a structure is arrested it would sooner or later topple over. Our cultivators cannot long continue to bear on their shoulders the yearly increasing burden of an expensive administration on the Western pattern and of the maintenance of an annually expanding unproductive upper class. Every civilised society from remote antiquity has favoured the growth of parasites. But modern society, is a veritable paradise of parasites.

The complexity of the machinery of the Government and its expenditure have been increasing apace. In 10 years, between 1901-2 and 1911-12, it rose from £59,681,619 to £78, 895,416. Since 1912, the complexity of gubernatorial machinery and consequent increase of expenditure have been going up by leaps and bounds, especially since the inauguration of the Montagu-Chelmsford Reform Scheme. Machinery is only a means to an end and that end is, or should be, the welfare of the people. Its value is to be tested by the amount of its contribution to that welfare. I know of no truth which is more obvious, but which, nevertheless, is more disregarded in Governmental circles, and in circles in any way connected with the Government.

They lavishly spend the hard-earned money of the multitude upon the expansion of multifarious departments without apparently making any inquiry as to whether the departments are doing them any good or not, whether while the machinery of the administration is being expanded and amplified after the Western fashion, the vast economic gulf which separates them from the Westerner is being bridged or not. The Government with its numberless departments and the prosperous classes of new India consisting of zamindars, lawyers, money-lenders, etc., may be compared to an immense reservoir fed by various channels through which flow the resources of the people. For the betterment of their condition one of two things is necessary—either the supply at the head must be increased, or the reservoir must be made shallower.

Not likely to be changed under Swara Government.

The recently published report of the "All Parties Conference" gives the most authoritative forecast of the Swaraj Government. We have hardly any indication in it of any substantial reduction in the consuming capacity of the reservoir. There are, on the contrary, indications of a considerable increase of that capacity. New provinces are to be created which means an addition to the high-salaried Governors with their usual paraphernalia of costly noodles and ornamental no-bodies. Then again great stress is laid upon mass education. Now let us see what "mass education" on a large scale would mean. According to the Census of 1921, there were in British India only 22,623,651 literates in vernaculars, the products of primary schools. The expenditure on these schools in 1920-21 amounted to Rs 4,53,53,627. For the accomplishment of the object of our political leaders to anything approaching tolerable satisfaction the expenditure would have to be increased very largely. The extra expenditure would have to be raised by taxation, which means that the incidence of taxation per head would have to be vastly increased. But there is a considerable body of weighty opinion that the limit of the capacity of our people to bear taxation has long since been reached. Sir C. A. Elliott observed when he was Settlement Officer, North-Western Provinces : "I do not hesitate to say that half our agricultural population never know from year's end to year's end what it is to have their hunger fully satisfied." Sir W. Hunter said in 1879, that "the fundamental difficulty of bringing relief to the Deccan peasantry is that the Government assessment does not leave enough food to the cultivator to support himself and his family throughout the year." He estimated that at least a fifth of our population lived on the brink of starvation. We have no evidence to show that matters have improved since the days of Elliott and Hunter. On the contrary, the greater frequency of famines, the enhanced indebtedness of the peasantry, and the increased ravages of disease tend to show that they have been going from bad to worse, and that the vitality of our people has been steadily diminishing. Any considerable addition to taxation would mean their bleeding to such an extent as to leave but little blood in them to enjoy Responsible Government when they get it. The Government would then be responsible to a community of paupers and imbeciles preyed upon by tax-gatherers and usurers.

We thus see, that there is no prospect of any attenuation of the capacity of the reservoir which is fed by the resources of the people. On the contrary, it is likely to be considerably deepened. Let us see what chance there is of augmentation of supply at the head. One of the measures strongly advocated by good many of my Neo-Indian compatriots is the adoption of a protective tariff for the development of Indian industries by Indian agency. But as the authors of the Montagu-Chelmsford scheme pointed out, the effect of high tariff would be, "that these industries will be largely financed by foreign capital attracted by the tariff." It is not foreign capital only that would be attracted, but foreign agency also, and the result of high tariff would probably be enhanced drain on the resources of the people for the benefit of foreigners. Foreign capital would be welcome only if it could be utilised by native agency. But there is no chance of that, as foreigners are not only immensely wealthier, but are also vastly superior in technical and commercial experience, and the report of the All-Parties Conference assures them that there is to be no "discriminating legislation against any community doing business lawfully in India."

Besides protective tariff, the measures which are advocated for industrial development on modern methods by indigenous agency are the spread of technical education and increased facilities for banking and credit.

During the last three decades private effort has enthusiastically co-operated with that of the Government, and various institutions for scientific and technical education have sprung up maintained by the State and by the munificence of public-spirited individuals. Besides, hundreds of our young men have been receiving technical training in Europe, America and Japan. But the result so far has been highly disappointing. Industrial development has, indeed, been going on apace lately, especially in regard to mineral resources, but it has been effected mainly by foreign capital and foreign agency. That the betterment of the material condition of India chiefly depends upon her industrial development by indigenous agency is now generally recognised by my countrymen. And I know many with whom this recognition has not been confined to speeches and writings, but has been translated into action. But their endeavours have generally ended in failure. I have tried to probe the causes of this failure. *

---

* Vide ante p. 136.

The most important among them is want of capital. There is but little of it available for industrial ventures on modern methods. The hoarded wealth of India is a myth. Western enterprise has been attended by numerous failures. In mining ventures I doubt if even ten per cent. of the propositions taken up prove successful. But the Westerners being immensely wealthy the loss is but little felt by them. What the loss of a few *lakhs* is to them, that of a few hundreds is to Indians. Industrial development on up-to-date methods is mainly a question of capital. It is hardly possible for one of the poorest communities in the world to compete successfully with some of the richest who, besides, have a century of technical knowledge and experience at their back, and are endowed with superior industrial qualities the result of the operation of physical and other causes for many long centuries.

Extension of technical education would no doubt provide employment for a number of young men in the technical services of the Government and in the subordinate establishments of the industries conducted by foreigners. But, under existing conditions, we cannot reasonably expect any large measure of industrial development by indigenous agency. It is sometimes asserted, "that Indian capital will be forthcoming once it is realised that it can be invested with security and profit in

India ; a purpose that will be furthered by the provision of increased facilities for banking and credit.'' I think the increased facilities would benefit the Westerners a great deal more than the Indians. The jute mills and the coal mines of Bengal, the petroleum wells of Burma, and various other industries have demonstrated that capital can be invested in them with as much security and profit as can be expected from any industries on modern methods. No Government could carry the demonstration further or guarantee greater security or larger profit ; yet, how much Indian capital has been invested in them ?

Four or five decades ago the industrial situation of Japan was similar to that of India. Within that period Indians, like the Japanese, have been receiving higher scientific and technical education. The former are not less intelligent than the latter ; if anything, they are probably more so. Why has Japan advanced industrially so fast, while India has lagged behind so sadly ? The main reason appears to me to be that the Japanese Government had no difficulty in discriminating between the Japanese and the foreigners. When it helped industrial development, it helped such development by Japanese agency. Would it be possible for our Swaraj Government to enact laws which would prevent foreigners from owning shares in the great Indian Banks, from acquiring "the right to work mines," and from becoming "members of the Stock Exchange," as the Japanese Government did in favour of the Japanese ? Just after the War with China, the Japanese Government saved the Industrial Bank of Japan from collapse by using a large portion of the Chinese indemnity in taking over the debentures of the Bank. Would it be possible for our Swaraj Government to secure such indemnity for India from any quarter, or to apply a large portion of it for the special benefit of Indians ?

Thus we find, that Swaraj with Dominion Status is not likely to lighten the excessively heavy burden of a costly bureaucracy under which our people suffer at present, or to improve their capacity to bear it.

III.

Repression. In regard to repressive policy, it should be observed that it is followed by nearly every Government even when it is national, in Russia, Italy, Spain, Yugo-Slavia, Greece, China, Mexico etc. There is no tyranny more terrible than that of the mob, especially of the Western mob with its highly developed bellicose propensities. If oligarchy chastises with "whips," democracy chastises with "scorpions." The horrors of the Reign of Terror of the French Revolution have been recently re-enacted in the Red Terror of

Bolshevist Russia.* And the end is not yet. The bitter animosity between the "Haves" and the "Havenots," and the militant attitude of the latter continue to gain in volume and intensity despite the palliative measures which are adopted from time to time. It is possible that this hostility may not in future be confined within the limits of the nation, and may not be restricted to the mild form of civil warfare called strike, but may break out in cataclysmal class warfare all over Europe, as Lenin the last great apostle of revolutionary socialism, expected. Already we find in Europe an echo of the scenes which occurred during the last years of democratic Greece :

"The poor governed the cities and had no means of living. The idea occured to them to despoil the rich. Rich and poor hated one another and fought one another. When the poor got the upper hand, they exiled the rich and confiscated their goods; often they even adopted these two radical measures—1. The abolition of debts, 2. A new partition of lands. The rich when they returned to power exiled the poor......No means were found of recon-

* Trotsky in his book "The Red Situation in Russia" shows how the "Soviet bureaucracy tyrannizes mercilessly over the working class arrogating to itself privileges which go further than those formerly held by the capitalist employers. The sovereignty of the people he declares, has become a fiction, all power being vested in the Stalin oligarchy."

ciling the two parties ; the rich could not persuade themselves to surrender their property ; the poor were unwilling to die of hunger. They fought savagely, as is always the case with neighbours."

Even in the United Kingdom which has to a great extent escaped from the evils infesting continental Europe owing to its insular position and comparative conservatism, hundreds of conscientious objectors were cast into prison during the great War, and Balbriggan did not fall far short of Jhallianwalla Bagh in atrocity. The treatment accorded to the Pacifists and the conscientious objectors during the late Great War was similar to what was meted out to the pro-Boers during the Boer War graphically described by Herbert Spencer :

"The temper generated by these causes (leading to militarism) has resulted in the outbursts of violence occuring all over England in the towns, large and small, where those who entertain opinions disliked by the majority respecting our treatment of the Boers, have been made the victims of mobs—mobs which not only suppressed even private meetings and ill-treated those who proposed to take part in them, kicking and even tarring them in the public streets, but attacked the premises of those who were known to be against the war, smashing shop-windows, breaking into houses, and even firing into them. And now after these breaches of the law continued for two years have been habitually condoned by the authorities, we find leading newspapers applauding the police for having judiciously refrained from interfering with the mob in its treatment of the stop-the-war speakers !

Surely a society thus characterized and thus governed is a fit habitat for hooligans."

That much-boomed land of freedom, the United States of America, within a year of the close of the Great War, became "engaged in an anti-socialist campaign, more sweeping, more ruthless, by any test which you care to apply—the numbers arrested, the severity of the sentences imposed, the nature of the offences alleged than anything ever attempted by Bismarck or the Kaiser. Old men of seventy (one selected by the socialist party as Presidential candidate) young girls, college students, are sent to prison with sentences of ten, fifteen or twenty years. The elected members of State Legislature are not allowed to sit on the ground of their socialist opinions. There are deportations in whole shiploads.........American marines. ...have killed as many Haytians as the Black and Tans have killed Irish. Nor for that matter, Americans know that every year there takes place in their own country—as there has taken place week after week in the years of peace for half a century—atrocities more ferocious than any which are alleged against even the British or the German. Neither of the latter burn alive weekly untried fellow-countrymen with a regularity that makes the thing an institution." *

* "The Fruits of Victory". By Norman Angell p.p. 156-157.

The Britons, in India no doubt, adopt stricter measures for securing their safety and that of their Government than what would have been the case had they been settled in the country and formed any considerable section of its population. Such a law as Act III of 1818 is, I believe, an anachronism in the case of any present-day national Government, and espionage in India is probably more systematic than elsewhere. Here is a case from my own experience. A young cousin of mine who associated with the Extremists during the period of the Bomb outrages in Bengal, and who was brought by me in 1908 to Ranchi, where I was then getting settled, was shadowed by a spy. My consin used to preach the Swadeshi cult in the town. But what was, perhaps, more objectionable in the eye of the police was that he used to collect the labourers employed in the building operations of my house in an *Akhra* and indulge in physical exercises with them. As I had to leave Ranchi for a time, I left instruction with him to have a sword such as is used for pruning hedges in these parts, and some other implements for gardening made by a blacksmith. The spy exaggerating this order and connecting it with his previous association with Extremists, the preaching of Swadeshi and the *Akhra* thought he would get kudos for having netted a dangerous revolutionary in my cousin. Fortunately, the blacksmith was honest enough to stick to his statement, that my cousin's order was only for some gardening implements, and he escaped. On the other hand, as Rector of the National Council of Education (which was in bad odour with Government) I was informed that I was watched by the police. But, though I criticised Government as freely as any member of the Congress, I always had a deeprooted aversion for and deprecated revolutionary methods of violence, and I never had any trouble. In fairness to Government, it should also be noted, that though in some cases their repressive measures partake of the nature of the Bengali saying "planting of guns for the killing of mosquitoes" they are at least partly justified by the fact that the party of violence, as we shall see in the next chapter, is not yet extinct.

Likely to continue under Swaraj Government.

Under Swaraj on the western model such repressive laws as act III of 1818, and the Ordinance of 1929 just passed by the Viceroy will no doubt be abrogated. But there are indications, that repression will continue. The late Surendra Nath Bannerji was long the idol of the youth but in his last days was execrated and even assaulted by them. If is not difficult to imagine what his fate and that of Moderates like him would have been had an Indian Demos been invested with the authority of Government.

Suppression of freedom of thought and of opinion, not un-often with more or less of force, is almost an every day occurence in the present day political world. Here is a case within my own experience. During the Non-Cooperation Movement, some of my fellow citizens did me the honour to ask me to become President of an organisation which would try to carry out its constructive programme—National Education, Removal of untouchability, Promotion of indigenous industry, and Temperance. I told them I was in whole-hearted sympathy with it, and that I would be glad to accept their offer if the organisation were not directly political and were called *Ranchi Hitasadhini Sabha* (Society for the promotion of the welfare of Ranchi). They agreed and organised a big mass meeting to inaugurate the society. Speeches advocating temperance, national education etc., in which the policy of the Government was adversely criticised were very favourably received. But as soon as an aged lawyer, a highly respected fellow-citizen, said that we are too apt to severely criticize the shortcomings of Government and to overlook those of our own organisations like our Municipality, he was hooted down. Up stood a young man on a bench and began to harangue about the defects of the Government which was vociferously cheered. There was in fact such an uproar, that the united efforts of the leaders failed to restore order, and I was obliged to close the meeting. The "Society for the Promotion of the welfare of Ranchi" died an abortive death despite the assurance that there would be no bar to its politically disposed members to join any political Association.

Repression under Imitation Swaraj may in some respects prove to be much more serious than at present. The nationalist Governments of Russia and China are relentlessly persecuting religions. Under Soviet rule, thousands of religious people and ministers of religion have been subjected to savage persecution, the express object of which has been to root religion out of the land. William Liebnicht, one of the prominent protagonists of Socialism, declares: "It is our duty as socialists to root out the faith in God with all zeal, nor is any one worthy of name who does not consecrate himself to the spread of atheism." Sometime ago it was reported, that a League of Communist youths in Russia had arranged processions with the object of destroying religious feeling, and had erected scaffolds in Petrograd and Moscow on which effigies of Christ and Virgin Mary were beheaded. The following account of recent iconoclasm in China is taken from the *Amrita Bazar Patrika* of Calcutta (March 17, 1929):

"Now in recent months a wave of hostility towards temples, monks, and idols has spread through the Kuomintang. It is one of the most curious phases of the new spirit in China, and its manifestations are worth recording. The first striking instance of it was reported in August from Haichow, in North Kiangsu. A few miles east of the city, at Nanchong, is a big and famous temple which the local Kuomintang determined to attack. The legend runs that the first three men who planned the campaign fell upon untimely disaster. But the Kuomintang leaders were not to be frightened. Providing themselves with a guard of soldiers as a protection against temporal enmities at least they went to the temple, lassoed the principal images, dragged them from the temple, and burnt them. Two other temples in the neighbourhood were treated in the same way. In one case there was a serious riot, and one of the reformers was badly hurt. But the Kuomintang stuck to their purpose, closed the temples, and declared their very considerable lands confiscated, the property to be used for educational purposes.

The next move occurred at Hanyang, at the great temple of the Nine Pure Ones. This temple is particularly frequented at the Mid-Autumn festival; but this year there were no celebrations. The Hupeh Government declared that no one was to go near the temple for a month, and put a guard of soldiers about it to enforce the order. No actual destruction was done. But a similar prohibition was enforced a few days later upon the pilgrimages to the Mu Lan Shan temple a few miles from Hankow. These pilgrimages have always been very popular during the first days of the eighth moon. In Imperial days large strings of boats would be seen going up the river, flying flags which announced that they carried pilgrims to the Mu Lan Shan, and these flags were a sufficient safeconduct alike with officials and outlaws. This year there were none. Here, again, no iconoclasm was attempted and confiscation of temple lands, though talked of, has not been carried out. But this is probably because the monks, being very big property owners, are also very good landlords, who care for their tenants assiduously; and the Kuomintang are probably frightened of the consequences of assaulting them.

Reports of similar action against temples have drifted through from several other districts, but not on a large scale. In one case the city Magistrate himself struck the first blow which was to decapitate the idol. Off flew the axe-head and in falling wounded the Magistrate's foot. Instantly the legend spread that the idol had wrested the axe from his hand and smitten its impious assailant dead. But the Magistrate lost no time in appearing about the streets to prove himself very much alive. "The dog it was that died"—or rather the idol, for another axe was obtained and the decapitation completed, according to plan.

Just before Christmas the Kuomintang executed a big raid in the Paoshan district, where the Whangpoo enters the Yangtze some 12 miles from Shanghai where there is one particularly well-known temple containing 60 or 70 images, besides numerous smaller fanes. All the shrines were ruthlessly attacked, images dragged from their pedestals, their heads hacked off and bodies sawn asunder. Whether there has been any confiscation of lands I have not heard, but it is to be expected.

Lastly, at Taichow, on the Chekiang coast, there was a big demonstration against the principal city temple on New Year's Day. The City Magistrate, chief of police, and local garrison commander, as well as the chief representatives of the Kuomintang, all took part. Speeches were made on such subjects as "Uselessness of Idols." "Superstition and Ignorance and their Ends." Three hours were thus spent in working up popular feeling in the approved way, and then a concerted move was made on the temple, all the images were hacked down and destroyed, and the doors locked and sealed, while the priests fled in terror."

Probable influence of communism under Swaraj Government.

The personality of Mahatma Gandhi, his compromising spirit, and the strong desire in our political world to present a united front of opposition to Government have for the time being prevented the Communist party to measure their strength with the Moderates who would be contented with Dominion Status. As soon, however, as Swaraj is established, they would be sure to struggle for supremacy and begin the nefarious work of revolutions and counter revolutions which have made such havoc in Russia and China. The fact is significant, that last January some 25,000 labourers are reported to have held a mass meeting in the Maidan of Calcutta and passed through the streets carrying flags and inscriptions stating, "Long live the Soviet Republic of India," "Down with the Landlord," "All power to the Masses," "Workers of the World unite," "Long Live Revolution in India."

The writer has elsewhere* dealt with the evils of socialism. "All Socialism" rightly says Herbert Spencer, "involves slavery," and he wrote before it developed into present-day Communism or Bolshevism. The possible prospect of exchanging our present bondage for the worse bondage of a Bolshevist Swaraj is by no means cheering. "We have never" said Lenin frankly, "spoken

* "Some Present-day Superstitions," Chapter II.

of liberty. We shall exercise the dictatorship until the majority submit." Trotsky also declared, that "democracy is a worthless and wretched masquerade. We repudiate it in the name of the proletariat. Three times hopeless is the idea of coming into power through democracy."

Concluding observations.

We thus find, that in regard to economic drain, the highly expensive character of administration, and repression, which are the three main defects of the existing alien government we are not likely to fare any better under Imitation Swaraj. And the following considerations weigh with us in considering the former to be a less serious evil than the latter. I agree with good many of my compatriots in considering the Montford Reforms to be but little better than veritable shams. I would rather have pure-bred, frank autocracy than this mongrel, camouflaged, dyarchic democracy with communal representation. The persistence, however, with which several apparently sincere well-wishers of India invite the co-operation of politically-minded Indians to make the Montford Reforms a success makes one so far charitably disposed as not to ascribe their genesis solely to cynicism and superlative British proficiency in diplomacy, but also, to some extent at least, to a most irrational, though quite natural bias in favour of the Western form of democracy.

The Morley-Minto Reforms which, like the Montagu-Chelmsford Reforms, were ushered in with a great flourish of trumpets as inaugurating a new era of Indian progress also savoured largely of the character of simulacra. But Lord Morley being one of the few highly cultured, honest, good souls who have drifted or been inveigled into the tortuous path of practical politics, took but little pains to conceal the fact, that they were purposely designed to rally and placate the docile,non-violent Moderates, and win their support against the intractable, bomb-throwing Extremists; and he emphatically declared that they were not meant to lead to the Parliamentary form of Government in India.

It is otherwise with the Montagu-Chelmsford Reforms. They have plunged our people into the whirlpool of ballot-box democracy, with but little of its good and with all its evil to which is to be added the special one of communal representation. The All Parties Conference suggest the abolition of communal electorates, but recommend universal adult suffrage. That would, we are afraid, be "jumping from the frying pan into the fire." The mischievous activities of dunder-headed windbags and shallow-pated scribblers would be increased a thousand fold. The vitriolic vituperations of the various parties into which Indian society is being divided would vastly increase in volume, in intensity, and in bitterness. Bribery and corruption in forms which elude the clutches of law would become immensely more rife. Assaults and broken limbs (if not broken heads) would become a much more marked feature of large political gatherings. The new variety of social pests of the same species as touts and pettifoggers in the form of political hucksters and mountebanks circulating lies and scandals and fomenting animosity and dissension which has of late been rising would greatly gain in number and influence. Human nature has not appreciably changed since the time of Aristophanes who described Demos as a besotted old man who is foolishly credulous, lets flatterers and intriguers pull him around by the nose, and is enraptured when they harangue. The chorus in one of his comedies addressing a charlatan says: "You are rude, vicious; you have a strong voice, an impudent eloquence, and violent gestures, believe me you have all that is necessary to govern Athens."

Then, again, it does not require any long stretch of imagination to foresee, that the spirit of truckling to the caprices and prejudices of our Moslem brethren, * which is evidenced

* As an instance of the desire to conciliate Mahomendan opinion at any cost may be given the burial sometime ago of a fakir in compliance with the unreasonable wishes of a rowdy Mahomedan mob by the Calcutta Municipality (which

by the pacts and compromises made by our political leaders (especially the pact which was made by the great leader of the Swarajya party who received the title of *Deshbandhu*) would be carried to the Swaraj Government, for, otherwise, it could not be established or maintained. Not only of the Moslems, but also

---

at the time was dominated by the Swarajya party) in the heart of the premier Municipal Market against Municipal and sanitary rules. The inquiries of a Municipal committee led to the conclusion that the Fakir in question "was an exconvict who afterwards became a menial servant, and eventually a non-descript loafer."

The conditions of the pact entered into by the Swarajya party with the Moslems "were divided into two groups,—political and religious. On the political side it was decided that (1) Representation in the Bengal Legislative Council would be on the basis of population. (2) Representation in the local bodies would be in the proportion of 60 to 40 viz., the majority community in a district would get 60 and the minority community 40 per cent. of seats in the district boards local boards, union boards and municipalities (3) 55 per cent. of the total number of Government posts would be permanently held by the Mussalmans and as the present percentage was far below that, they would continue to receive 80 per cent every year till that 55 per cent was made up. These three were the main political concessions. As to the religious concessions, the pact enjoined that the Hindus should show toleration by (1) not allowing music in processions before any mosque (2) not interfering with the killing of cows for sacrifice (3) not supporting any legislative measure in the Council for the prohibition of killing cows for food." (*The Statesman*).

of the Communists and the socalled "depressed classes," who too have been clamouring for a share in the legislatures and the services proportionate to their numercial strength.

To placate all these sections of our community and reconcile their conflicting interests, the Swaraj Government would have to cast to the winds, all considerations of equity, merit and efficiency. The capable, the good and the wise who form a microscopic minority of the community would be swamped, if not wiped out, in the cut-throat scramble for official preferments. Swaraj under these conditions would be one of the most inept, invertebrate, chaotic forms of hare-brained mob rule the world has ever seen.

CHAPTER VIII.

IS POLITICAL SWARAJ POSSIBLE?

Methods of Violence —the Sepoy War.

For nearly a century, political India has been divided into two parties, one advocating representative Government after the Western fashion and partnership in the British Empire as the ideal, and constitutional means as the method of its attainment, and the other aspiring to complete independence by violent methods. The efforts of the latter culminated in the Sepoy War. They never had, and are never likely to have a better chance. The Sepoys were nearly as well equipped, armed, and drilled as their antagonists. The dictum of Sir Thomas Munro, that if civilization were "to become an article of trade between England and India," the former "would gain by the import cargo"—still held good. The modern industrial civilization of the West had not as yet made much progress in India. Not more than two hundred miles of railway had as yet been opened to traffic. Malaria, Kalajar, tuberculosis, and an infinity of other ailments, and the Arms Act &c. had not yet begun to sap the vitality and virility of the manhood of India. The village Self-Government had not yet been sufficiently suppressed to make the people lose their self-reliance and self-respect. Above all, intercommunal amity still prevailed among the Hindus, the Moslems and the "untouchables."

Conspiracies of Revolutionaries.

The failure of the Sepoy War to secure Swaraj practically gave the quietus to the party of physical force. But the party is not extinct. The more ardent and intransigent of our intelligentsia have absolutely no faith in the only weapons, the pen and the tongue, which are wielded by the party of non-violent constitutional agitation. They first came into great prominence in Bengal under the designation of "Extremists" over two decades ago. They conspired together and manufactured bombs in a suburb of Calcutta (Maniktala). The conspiracy was discovered by Government in 1908 leading to the arrest of a number of young men, and in the course of their trial the approver was assassinated. This led Government to have recourse to rigorous measures for the suppression of the terrorist movement, which aspired to attain Swaraj by bombs and revolvers. Not only were the young men directly implicated in the Manicktola conspiracy and the murders which followed it severely punished in the ordinary course of Law, but several leaders who had no connection whatever with them and were merely suspected of anti-Government tendencies were arrested and deported under Regulation III of 1818.

Since 1910, the terrorist party was, for sometime, in a state of suspended animation, and their obscure, fugitive existence was only inferred from occasional bomb outrages and from intercepted correspondence with Bolshevik agents. Latterly, however, they again appear to have been coming into prominence. "Early in 1924, branches of a revolutionary organisation calling itself the Hindustan Republican Association were formed in various places in the United Provinces, the object of which was the establishment of a socalled 'Federated Republic of the United States of India.' This was to be achieved by means of an armed rebellion, and to this end it was decided to collect funds in as many ways as possible, including the use of force and the commission of crime. In furtherance of the common object of this Association, certain of its members committed crimes in the United Provinces and distributed revolutionary literature there and in other provinces. All the crimes were accomplished by violence and murder, and in one of them brutal torture was used. In the last crime of the series, an armed docoity committed on the night of the 9th August, 1925, over Rs 4,600 in cash and currency notes was plundered from the cash chests in the guard's van of a train travelling from Moradabad to Lucknow, just a little way outside the Kakori Railway Station, and one person was killed." *

* India in 1926—27. p 286.

A similar conspiracy was discovered at Deogarh in the province of Bihar and Orissa in 1927. And as I am writing this (April, 1929), news comes from Delhi of a dastardly bomb-outrage in the Legislative Assembly. Along with the bombs, there fell copies of a red leaflet signed by Balraj glòrying in the title of "Commander-in-Chief of the Hindusthan Socialist Republican Army" :—

"It takes a loud voice to make the deaf hear." With these immortal words uttered on a similar occasion by a valiant French Anarchist Martyr, do we strongly justify this act of ours. Without repeating the humiliating history of the past ten years of the working of the reforms and without mentioning the insults hurled down upon the head of the Indian Nation through this House the so-called Indian Parliament —we want to point out that while the people are expecting some more crumbs of reforms from the Simon Commission, and are even quarrelling over the distribution of the expected bones, Government is thrusting upon us new repressive measures like those of the Public Safety and Trade Disputes Bills while reserving the Press Sedition Bill for the next session.

Indiscriminate arrests of labour leaders working in the open field clearly indicate whither the wind blows. In these extremely provocative circumstances, the Hindustan Socialist Republican Association, in all seriousness, and realising its full responsibility, decided and ordered its Army to do this particular action so that a stop be put to this humiliating farce and to let the alien Bureaucratic exploiters do what they wish, but to make them come before the public eye in their naked form.

"Let the representatives of the people return to their constituencies and prepare the masses for the coming revolution and let Government know that, while protesting against the Public Safety and Trade Disputes Bills and the callous murder of Lala Lajpat Rai on behalf of the helpless Indian masses, we want to emphasise the lesson often repeated by history that it is easy to kill individuals but you cannot kill ideas. Great empires crumbled while ideas survived; Bourbons and Czars fell, while revolutions marched triumphantly ahead.

"We are sorry to admit that we, who attach so great sanctity to human life, we, who dream of a very glorious future when man will be enjoying perfect peace and full liberty, have been forced to shed human blood. But the sacrifice of individuals at the altar of a revolution that will bring freedom to all, rendering exploitation of man by man impossible is inevitable. Long live Revolution."

This nefarious work is ascribed to Bolshevist influence. A Bolshevik conspiracy was discovered in 1924, The well known communist M. N. Roy had been engaged in organising in India a conspiracy on behalf of the Third Communist International. "British Rule, Government by upper and middle class Indian alike were to be swept away, the consfiscation of property was to be wholesale. A 'People's party' was to be the initial step, having a public programme designed for their betterment which in no way offended against the law. Within that apparently harmless body 'illegal' activities were to be prosecuted by an inner party consisting of all the revolutionary nationalities. Violence and destruction of property were to be encouraged, and conflicts to be precipitated. At the propitious moment, resources and armed help were to come from the 'universal revolutionary party' i. e. the Communist International......In the event of the overthrow by force of arms of the British Government, the revolutionaries proposed to sweep away all Indian political groups and labour organisations which did not come into line. The power of upper and middle class Indian was to be destroyed by taking from them all that they possessed." *

The terrorist organisations whether indigenous or inspired by Bolshevism are as likely to succeed in their object of overturning the British Rule with bombs and revolvers as Dame Partington was in staying the flood of the Atlantic with her mop and broom. One cannot, however, help admiring the immense self-sacrifice and the indomitable courage displayed by some of the revolutionaries, and commiserating them on the tragic consequences of their misguided patriotism. Apart from the futility of their methods of violence they have a highly pernicious influence upon our society. In the case of Ireland, Mr. P. S. O' Hegarty rightly observes in his "Victory of Sinn Fein" :

"We devised certain 'bloody instructions' to use against the British. We adopted political assassination as a principle ; we devised the ambush ; we encouraged women to forget their

---

* "India in 1924—25"—pp. 100—101.

sex and play at gunmen ; we turned the whole thoughts and passions of a generation upon blood and revenge and death ; we placed gunmen, mostly half-educated and totally inexperienced, as dictators with powers of life and death over large areas. We derided the Moral Law and said there was no law but the law of force. And the Moral Law answered us. Every devilish thing we did against the British went its full circle and then boomeranged and smote us tenfold ; and the cumulative effect of the whole of it was a general moral weakening, and a general degradation, and a general cynicism and disbelief in either virtue or decency, in goodness, or uprightness, or honesty. The Irregulars drove patriotism, and honesty, and morality out of Ireland. They fouled all the wells, and made the task of saving Ireland tenfold harder than it had been."

II

Failure of Non-violent Non-Co-operation.

The method of Non-violent Non-cooperation for the attainment of Swaraj was adopted by the Indian National Congress about a decade ago at the initiative of Mahatma Gandhi. It failed as it was bound to. Under existing conditions, it must remain a noble ideal reducible to practice only in a small way. It was hardly consonant with reason to extend it to high politics. Constituted as the nature of man has been since he left the cave and began to lead a social life, a certain amount of moral obliquity is inevitable in politics.

In the Bhagavatgita, Srikrishna stills the rebellious voice of Arjuna's conscience by assuring him that as a Kshatriya, it was his duty to fight for his rights and not spare his relations if necessary; and, if the Mahabharat is to be trusted, the divine charioteer condoned or connived at, if not countenanced such deviations from the straight path of righteousness as are inevitable in warfare. There are numerous legends which show that even the Gods were by no means strangers to the dark and tortuous ways of diplomacy. I shall give one. The Devas persuaded a Sage named Dadhichi to sacrifice himself so that his bones might be utilised for making that invincible weapon of warfare called "Vajra." His son, however, vowing vengeance, performed "tapasya," as a result of which there emerged from his thigh a fire-demon (Varabanala), who threatened to consume all the Devas. Vishnu, the protecting deity, shrewdly advised the demon to take them piece-meal, and first of all, destroy the chief among them, the Ocean. The latter agreed, but asked for a guide as he did not know the way. The goddess Sarasvati was deputed for the purpose, and after sundry adventures led him safely to the Ocean. The demon was so pleased with her services that he offered to confer a boon on her ; and the boon she asked for was that he should consume the Ocean with his mouth so contracted as not to exceed the point of a needle. Thus were the the gods saved from one of the greatest catastrophes they had ever been threatened with by a piece of celestial stratagem, which a Machiavelli and a Bismarck would have envied.

Leaving mythology aside, and coming to the "terra firma" of history, the monotony of its loathsome record of the feats of glorified swindlers, brigands, assassins and murderers, is relieved by the humanitarian deeds of a few high-principled sovereigns. Among the most notable of these were Asoka Priyadarsi and Marcus Aurelius. But the former had had his fill of blood and had been securely established on the throne before he became a convert to the humane cult of Gautama Buddha and proclaimed "Ahinsa," and the latter did not find it inconsistent with the noble sentiments treasured in his "Meditations" to vigorously prosecute military expeditions, or actively persecute troublesome people like the Christians. Sivaji was a very pious monarch. He placed his kingdom at the feet of his Guru, Ramdas. The latter, however, very wisely declined the offer. In recent times, men of strict integrity have occasionally drifted or been inveigled into the political sphere. But, they have either had to become doublefaced, or had to be elbowed out or relegated to positions in which their squeamishness would not stand in the way of their less pachy-dermatous colleagues. Honest John Bright was one of the most conspicuous among such men, and he could not be trusted with situations of any greater responsibility than that of President of the Board of Trade, or of Chancellor of the Duchy of Lancaster, and even as such, he had to appeal to his constituents to remember that he was "now one man serving in a band of men, no longer responsible only for himself, no longer independent of the acts of others."

Non-violent Non-Cooperation was unquestionably a brilliant idea. Formerly there were two parties—the Moderates, the Party of Constitutional agitation, petition and prayer, and the Extremists who advocated physical force in one form or another. There was no middle course between mendicancy and violence. Non-violent Non-Co-operation instilled the idea into a good number of our politicals, that they would have to depend entirely upon their own efforts. It involved neither begging nor violence, could be carried out without any shock to self-respect or breach of moral rule, and is eminently suited to people so pacifically and spiritually disposed as ours. Under existing conditions, however, it cannot be expected to be successful except in the case of a small community the members of which keenly feel that they are suffering an intolerable wrong at the hands of a section of the bureaucracy, or of a party favoured by the bureaucracy. One of the most striking instances of such successful resistance that occurs to me was that offered by the peasantry of certain districts of Bengal in the sixties of the last century. They were compelled by British indigo planters to sow indigo on their best lands, failing which they were severely oppressed. When their sufferings exceeded the bounds of their patience (of which they have an unusually good share), they took the vow that they would never grow indigo again. "The planters got furious. They arrested the ring leaders and tortured them in an atrocious manner. The huts of the rayats were razed to the ground. A large number of them were confined and maltreated in the dreary indigo godowns ; the vast majority of them were rendered homeless, and they and their wives and children wandered all over the country without food or shelter. But they would not yield. The planters now got alarmed and changed their tactics ; with the help of the officials they sought to conciliate the leaders of the movement. Better terms and ample compensation were offered to them, but all in vain. One cry they had raised and they stuck to it to the last—"Saheb this hand shall never touch indigo again." The District Magistrates and Divisional Commissioner then interfered—they promised justice and protection to the rayats. They threatened and coaxed them in turn, but to no purpose. 'Sow the seed only this season,' was the last request of a District

Magistrate ; 'Saheb, we have taken the vow, we shall never break it and sully our soul ; torture we don't mind, our hands shall never again touch indigo.' And as a matter of fact, they never touched it again with the result that the planters had to go away leaving their palatial buildings behind.

The passive resistance of the peasantry of Champaran, Kaira and Bardoli against Zamindars and Government was also successful. In all these instances, however, the success was probably due as much to an apprehension by Government of such resistance ultimately developing into mob violence as to a sense of justice.

The adoption of the principle of non-violent non-co-operation by the National Congress which challenged the authority, if not the very existence in India of one of the most powerful European peoples of the present day was a very bold idea, but was hardly justifiable. It was hardly reasonable to expect, that a people whose nature is such as, in the words of Herbert Spencer, "has filled Europe with millions of armed men, here eager for conquest, there for revenge," "which prompts the nations called Christian to vie with one another in filibustering expeditions all over the world regardless of the claims of aborigines", and "which in dealing with weaker peoples goes beyond the primitive rule of life for life, and for one life takes many lives," a people who associate greatness with successful violence so that they erect statues in prominent places to masters of it, while the good and the wise die "unhonoured, unwept and unsung," it was, hardly reasonable to expect that such a people would yield to non-violent soul force. Not to speak of strikes of working men, which sometimes assume the magnitude of civil wars, even cultured ladies in England had recourse to bomb and other outrages in order to obtain from their own kith and kin what they consider to be their rights. Soul-force is a weapon which is not at all likely to tell on a people like this, especially when the question is one of "to be or not to be." On the contrary, it is rather calculated to excite their contempt. Mohatma Gandhi's own experience should have taught this. In South Africa he cordially helped the British in their war with the Boers, which was pronounced by not a few of their own thinkers as unrighteous and which was attended by manifold barbarities and atrocities, in the hope that they when successful would better the position of his compatriots. I need hardly say how very disappointing the result has been. Then, again, it was hardly resonable to expect, that in the present state of acute communal conflict, the majority of the heterogeneous mass of Indians, with divergent interests, and without any definite, tangible wrong so very serious and intolerable as would make them move and suffer with one mind, like the indigo rayats of Bengal or the peasantry of Bardoli would practise non-co-operation against a strong and powerful Government.

The amazing success of the Non-cooperation movement for two or three years was due mainly to Mahatma Gandhi's promise of Swaraj within a year or so which coming from a man of his saintly reputation had great weight with the credulous public. It was no doubt conditional upon the execution of his programme :—

1. Cultivating the spirit of non-violence. 2. Setting up Congress organisations in every village. 3. Introducing the spinning wheel in every home and manufacturing all the cloth required for our wants through the village weaver. 4. Collecting as much money as possible. 5. Promoting Hindu-Moslem Unity. 6. Ridding Hinduism of the curse of untouchability and otherwise purifying ourselves by avoiding intoxicating drinks and drugs.

But how the Mahatma could reasonably expect the carrying out of such a colossal programme within one year passes our comprehension. To our mind even one generation would be too short a time for its execution.

III.

Constitutional Agitation for Swaraj on Dominion status.

Indian political activities are now mainly confined to the advocates of non-violent constitutional agitation. However they may disagree among themselves, they just now agree in their goal which is authoritatively declared by the All parties Conference presided over by Pundit Motilal Nehru to be "Swaraj with dominion status," which implies equal partnership with the other members of the British Empire. Considering the treatment which is meted out to our fellow countrymen in the Colonies and Dominions, and not unoften even in India * by the Briton, and how the Oriental is generally regarded by the Occidental, the hope of such a consummation is hardly consonant with reason.

* "On almost every railway journey," observes Mr. H. W. Nevinson, "one sees instances of ill-manners that would appear too outrageous for belief at home. But it is the same throughout. In hotels, clubs, bungalows, and official chambers, the people of the country, especially the educated classes, are treated with a habitual contumely more exasperating than savage persecution." "Among women" says Sir H. J. S. Cotton, "who are more rapidly demoralised than men, the abuse of those 'horrid natives' is almost universal. Among men how often do we hear the term 'nigger' applied without any indication of anger or intentional contempt, but as though it were the proper designation of the people of the country! Even with those who are too well informed to use this term, the sentiment that prompts its use is not

The operation of physical and psychical causes during untold generations has produced in the Briton sundry qualities which are different from those which the same causes, have developed in the Indian. The former for mere animal existence maintained a fierce struggle against Nature for thousands of years in a way to which the latter were utter strangers, and are consequently much more combative, active, energetic, presevering, resolute, selfish, and greedy, and much less peace-loving, meditative, introspective, benevolent and unselfish. But such incompatibility of character and temperament is not necessarily a bar to partnership. The woman, for instance, has generally a sounder heart, but a weaker head than man. Yet they often live in happy, life-long, conjugal partnership. But one condition is essential

---

wholly set aside ....It is a grave symptom that the official body in India has now succumbed as completely as the non-official to anti-native prejudices.........It is indeed a grave position to which we have drifted, for the change is complete, and the tension acute. ("New India" pp 47—51) A Japanese diplomatist is reported to have said addressing a European audience.

"For two thousand years we kept peace with the rest of the world, and were known to it by the marvels of our delicate ethereal art, and the finely wrought productions of our ingenious handicrafts, and we were accounted barbarians. But from the day on which we made war on other nations and killed many thousands of our adversaries. you at once admit our claim to rank among civilized nations."

therefor—mutual sympathy, respect, and confidence. It is, however, notoriously wanting as between the Briton and the Indian. The qualities which the Indians generally excel in, and their culture, and ideals not only do not call for the sympathy or respect from the average Westerner, but are even looked down upon with but little disguised contempt. He views the mass of the Indians and other non-Westerners as so many objects to be exploited, or, at best, to be "civilized" in his own way, so that they may be effectively exploited. They could not command his respect uuless like the Japanese, they became a great military nation, or unless he underwent such ethical transformation as would change his view-point and his outlook on humanity. There is no sign of either at present.

No doubt, there are a few broad-minded, high-souled Englishmen like Sir C. Trevelyan, A. O. Hume, Wedderburn, Hyndman and Morley who sincerely sympathise with the Indians. But, in the first place, opinion is divided among them as to the suitability of Western democracy for India. Morley, for instance, certainly the most philosophical and cultured among them, declared emphatically that if his "existence, either officially or corporeally, were prolonged twenty times longer than either of them is likely to be, Parliamentary system in India is not the goal to which" he "for one moment would aspire." Secondly, they all contemplate an indefinite prolongation of Western tutelage for India which has, on the whole, been far more injurious than beneficial to her in a variety of ways, and which, if prolonged, would still further incapacitate her for beneficent self-government. Thirdly, they count but little in practical politics. It is men of the type of Birkenhead, Joynson Hicks, Crew, Sydenham and Baldwin that do. When they talk of the British Empire as a commonwealth, they always have in view, a commonwealth of Nations, with British, or at least European blood.

"Is it conceivable," asks Lord Crew, "that any time an Indian Empire could exist on the lines of Australia and New Zealand, with no British officials and troops, no tie of creed, or of blood replacing those material bonds?" "In India," says Lord Sydenham, "constitution-making is not studied, and I have been sometimes surprised to see colonial self-government advocated as a simple and natural devlopment capable of early realization. I wonder if those who hold these views have any idea of what colonial self govornment means." "I am not able," opines Lord Birkenhead, "in any foreseeable future to discern a moment when we may safely either to ourselves or India abandon our trust."

The cant of doing good to the people in the Dependencies and "spheres of influence" which some British Imperialists occasionally indulge in has been humorously described by Shadwell in the following lines :—

"If you see an island shore
Which has not been grabbed before,
Lying in the track of trade as islands should,
With the simple native quite
Unprepared to make a fight,
Oh, you just drop in and take it for his good,
Not for love of money be it understood.
But you row yourself to the land,
With a Bible in your hand,
And you pray for him and rob him ! for his good :
If he hollers, then you shoot him for his good.

* * * *

In India there are bloody sights
Blotting out the Hindu's rights,
Where wev'e slaughtered many millions for their good
And with bullet and with brand,
Desolated all the land,
But you know we did it only for their good,
Yes, and still more far away
Down in China, let us say
Where the "Christian" robs the "heathen" for his good,
You may burn and you may shoot,
You may fill your sack with loot,
But be sure you do it only for his good.

MORAL.

If you dare commit a wrong
On the weak because you're strong,
You may do it if you do it for his good.
You may kill him if you do it for his good."

Herbert Spencer writing in the beginning of the current century concludes a remarkable essay on "Re-Barbarization' with the following significant words :

"Thus on every side we see the ideas and feelings and institutions appropriate to peaceful life replaced by those appropriate to fighting life. In all places, and in all ways there has been going on during the last fifty years a recrudescence of barbaric ambitions, ideas and sentiments, and an unceasing culture of blood thirst. If there needs a striking illustration of the result, we have it in the dictum of the people's Laureate, that the 'lordliest life on earth' is one spent in seeking to 'bag certain of our fellowmen'."

Another eminent scientific observer, Alfred Russell Walace, writing about the same time as Herbert Spencer says :

"The latter half of the century (the nineteenth century) has witnessed a revival of the war spirit throughout Europe, which region has now become a vast camp, occupied by opposing forces greater in number than the world has ever seen before....And what a horrible mockery is all this when viewed in the light of either Christianity or advancing civilization ! All these nations armed to the teeth, and watching stealthily for some occasion to use their vast armaments for their own aggrandisement and for the injury of their neighbours are Christian nations. The state of things briefly indicated in this chapter is not progress but retrogression. It will be held by the historian of the future to show, that we of the nineteenth century were morally and socially unfit to possess and use the enormous powers for good or evil which the rapid advance of scientific discovery had given us ; that our boasted civilization was in many respects a mere surface veneer, and that our methods of Government were not in accordance with either Christianity or civilization. It has been often said that companies have no souls, and the same is still more true of the governments of our day."

There are also other, broad-minded benevolent Britons who sincerely deplore and protest against the nefarious military and predatory developments of their nation. But they not only do not count in practical politics, but such contemptuous epithets as "mugwumps," "rotters" etc. are showered upon them, and they are sometimes even persecuted both by the Government and the people. The British national character does not apper to have changed for the better since Herbert Spencer wrote half a century ago :—

> "In China, India, Polynesia, Africa, the East Indian Archipelago, reasons—never wanting to the aggressor—are given for widening our empire : without force if it may be, and with force if needful..... Be it in the slaying of the Karen tribes who resist Surveyors of their territory, or be it in the demand made on the Chinese in pursuance of the doctrine that a British traveller, sacred wherever he may choose to intrude shall have his death avenged on some one, we every where find pretexts for differences which lead to acquisitions. In the House of Commons and in the press the same spirit is shewn. During the debate on the Suez Canal purchase, our Prime Minister referring to the possible annexation of Egypt, said that the English people wishing the empire to be maintained 'will not be alarmed if it be extended,' and was cheered for so saying. And recently urging that it was time to blot out Dahomey the weekly organ of filibustering Christianity, exclaims—'Let us take Whydah and leave the Savage to recover it."

To expect Swaraj with Dominion Status by non-violent constitutional agitation from such a nation is hardly within the bounds of possibility.

Mr. Allan O Hume speaking at a farewell meeting at Bombay, in March 1894 is reported to have remarked as follows about political parties in England and what India may expect of them : "The great bulk of the leading politicians on both sides, the professional politicians as one may designate them, the men who mostly compose our Ministers, however virtuous, honest and upright they may be in private life, are in public life the veriest humbugs—talking like angels, but ready ever to do the devil's work—to sacrifice principle to party, and justice to those who are weak and politically dumb, as India is, to the exigencies of party political warfare. These Ministerial gangs are, as a body—of course there are exceptions—absolutely devoid of conscience and of any fixed principle except that of retaining place and power for themselves and friends and preventing the other side from enjoying any share of these....So then whenever the party in power is at all in a difficult position, sits weakly in the saddle and feels that it could easily be ejected there is scarely any conceivable in justice to India, or any other non-combatant party or region, of which it would not be guilty if it saw its way thereby to retain any wavering, or secure any new supporters."

Thus we find, that, under existing conditions, political Swaraj, even if it were desirable, is not practicable whether by violent or by non-violent methods. Concluding observations.

The efforts made for its attainment, therefore, appear to me to be more or less futile, and the time, energy, health and resources spent upon them are, to a great extent at least, wasted. I venture to suggest that it would be much wiser for us to take the existing Government as an unavoidable reality, and endeavour to minimise its evils so far as possible. In fact, I am strongly inclined to think that the traits of national character which have been developed in the Britishers by the age-long operation of physical and psychical causes, especially the military and sanguinary spirit and all that it connotes, make them admirably fit for a present-day Government with the annually increasing influence of diabolism all over the world.

Truth so seldom penetrates through the thick cloud of diplomatic verbiage and rodomontade, that we should rather be thankful than otherwise to have an occasional glimpse of it. And the candid utterances of men like Birkenhead and Joynson Hicks * instead of raising a violent tornado of indignation as they do in political India should rather produce the serener atmosphere of disillusionment. The British sword in its bare bald, naked

---

* "We did not conquer India" says Sir W. Joynson Hicks, "for the benefit of the Indians. I know it is said in Missionary meetings that we conquered India to raise the level of Indians. That is cant. We conquered India as the outlet for the goods of Great Britain. We conquered India by the sword, and by the sword we should hold it."

"The fundamental fact in the Indian situations" observes Lord Birkenhead, "is that we went to India centuries ago for composing with the sharp edge of the sword the differences which would have submerged and destroyed Indian Civilization. We went there on that basis and hold it by that charter."

form is such an unpleasant, loathsome, repulsive sight that we are apt to avert our eyes from it. We should, therefore, be rather grateful than otherwise to these candid gentlemen for pointedly reminding us of the presence of the hideous, relentless monster. Alas ! there it sits firmly supported by the "steel frame" of the Civil Service grinning and mocking at my deluded Swaraj-aspiring compatriots brandishing the only weapons of offence and defence they possess, the pen and the tongue, or fulminating futile threats of mass civil disobedience.*

* "We may surmise," says Dean Inge, "that the European man, the fiercest of all beasts of prey, is not likely to abandon the weapons which have made him the lord and bully of the planet. He has no other superiority to the races he arrogantly despises. Under a regime of peace, the Asiatic would probably be his master."

CHAPTER IX.

REVIVAL OF CULTURAL SWARAJ : DIFFICULTIES.

In the preceding chapters we have endeavoured to show, that the primary bond of Indian nationhood has hitherto been cultural; that India's swaraj from remote antiquity has been cultural rather than political; that this cultural swaraj which made her, on the whole, prosperous survived down to the earlier years of British Rule; that its decay since then is due to the supersession of the principles of Indian by those of Western culture in New India; that as a result of this supersession New India has been pursuing the path of Western Civilization; that this pursuit has contributed to the destruction of genuine village self-government, and the decay of indigenous industry and of communal concord;* and that the striving for political swaraj on the Western model, which is a result of this pursuit, is futile, because even if desirable, it is not possible.

---

* The writer has in his works "Some Present day Superstitions" and "Survival of Hindu civilization pt 2" shown how the pursuit of the path of Western Civilization has led to physical and moral degeneration.

Revival of Cultural Swaraj—objections from Politicals.

The salvation of India depends upon the revival of her Cultural Swaraj, which would necessitate our halting on the path of Western civilization, if not retracing our steps, to some extent at least. But the majority of my Neo-Indian brethren would ask—is that desirable ? Those among them who are politically disposed would aver, that if we went back to the ways of our ancestors, what would the Westerners think of us ? As it is, they take us to be barbarians ; if we did that, they would take us to be hopeless, incorrigible barbarians, constitutionally incapable of "progress." Some would say frankly, that "even professing ourselves to be their proteges, and loudly proclaiming the pride we take in being such, even becoming "Time-servers", "Two-tongues", and "Facing-both-ways," we have to rend the skies with plaintive cries and obstreperous objurgations to move our earthly Providence, the Government. If we fell in their estimation, even such favours as are now occasionally granted would be denied to us." My answer is, that it is better to be healthy and happy, and be branded as "barbarians" and "unprogressive," than be diseased and miserable and eulogised as "civilized" and "progressive," and that self-respect and self-reliance accord better with manliness, and, in the long run, do more good than subserviency and mendicancy. Then, again, what are the favours political India has got ? Lord Cross' Reforms of 1892, then the Morley-Minto Reforms, and last of all the Montagu-Chelmsford Reforms. Are they worth while? Have they made the mass of the people any happier ? Have they not rather added to the heavy burden of parasite-dom which they have to bear on their Atlantean shoulders ? The reforms are steps towards a form of Democracy which, in the words of Balfour is "almost played out [in modern Europe] ···and is fit only for Turkey or China." And for this precious boon my political compatriots have cooperated with Government to sacrifice indigenous democracy,* disseminate communal discord, and further the decay of indigenous industry !

As in the case of the individual, so in that of the community, the cultural, especially

---

* *Vide ante* Chapter IV. Mr. R. H. Elliott observes (*Fraser's* Magazine, April, 1872), "in former times there existed in India reigning powers that lived on the resources of the people, but...the internal management of affairs was left to the village communities, and the people had the power of modifying their customs in accordance with what seemed to them to be expedient. Now this power we have entirely taken away from them, and not only have we done this, but we thrust our meddling nose into all the details of life, and refine here and reform there, and always it must be remembered, with increased and unceasing taxation,......and we need hardly add that the results of this entire deprivation of free action are altogether deadly and destructive to the very existence of the most valuable powers of man."

ethical development has a much higher survival value than material or political progress. There are only two civilizations which have survived the wreck of the civilizations of antiquity—the Chinese and the Indian. And I have shown elsewhere, that this survival is attributable to their cultural, especially ethical development.*

The thinkers of the West are generally in agreement with the sages of India in subordinating political to other forms of individual or social activity. They know very well—

> " How small, of all that human hearts endure,
> That part which kings or laws can cause or cure."

Socrates considered himself to be "too upright a man to be safe" in politics.

"Forms of government" says Herbert Spencer "are valuable only where they are products of national *character*. No cunningly devised political arrangements will of themselves do anything. No amount of knowledge respecting the uses of such arrangements will suffice.........In proof I might enumerate the illustrations that lie scattered through the modern histories of Greece, of South America, of Mexico. Or I might dwell on the lesson.........presented us in France, where the political cycle shows us again and again that new Democracy is but old Despotism differently spelt, where now, as heretofore, we have *Liberte*, *Egalite*, *Fraternite*, conspicuous on the public buildings, and now, as heretofore, have for interpretations of these words the extremest party-hatreds, vituperations, and actual assaults in the Assembly, wholesale

---

* *Vide* "Epochs of Civilization," Ch. III.

arrests of men unfriendly to those in power, forbiddings of public meetings, and suppressions of journals ; and where now, as heretofore, writers professing to be ardent advocates of political freedom, rejoice in those acts which shackle and gag their antagonists" *

" The worth of a state, in the long run," says John Stuart Mill, "is the worth of the individuals composing it ; .... a state which dwarfs its men, in order that they may be more docile instruments in its hands even for beneficial purposes, will find that with small men no great thing can really be accomplished ; and that the perfection of machinery to which it has sacrificed every thing, will in the end avail it nothing, for want of the vital power which, in order that the machine might work more smoothly it has preferred to banish." †

The comparative futility of political activity is shown by the failure of the Western System of Representative Government which raised such extravagant expectations a century ago. We have just seen how, in the opinion of Herbert Spencer, it has failed in France. Dr. Jacks, Editor of the Hibbert Journal, observes :

"The professional politics of America are corrupt and debased to an extraordinary degree.........As things now are America is not a self-governing country except in name. The power behind the government is the political machine, which is controlled by the "bosses" and has become a veritable tyranny. The machine is a contrivance of remarkable ingenuity which can only be compared with the inventions of Edison, and its object is simply that of depriving free men of

* "The study of sociology," p. 276.

† "Liberty," Ch. V.

free use of their votes. I came in contact everywhere with men who groan under its tyranny."

In Great Britain, Mr. H. G. Wells observes:

"We do not have any Elections any more; we have Rejections. What really happens at a general election is that the party organisations—obscure and secretive conclaves with entirely mysterious funds,—appoint about twelve hundred men to be our rulers, and all that we, we so-called *self-governing* people, are permitted to do is, in a muddled angry way, to strike off the names of about half of these selected gentlemen."

A writer in the *North American Review* observed during the last great war "What are the millions of French, Austrian and Russian (and also Italian and German) boys in the trenches to-day but slaves? What have they ever been but slaves? Taken almost from the cradle and gripped by a system which held them as in a vice to become what? Cogs in a machine, a fighting machine, constructed with ruthless energy and superlative skill to beat down another fighting machine; nothing less, nothing more. Patriotism? Faugh!...............slavery? Compared with theirs ours which we abolished by war was beneficent and kindly."

Despite the opinions of Herbert Spencer and numerous other great thinkers of the West about the comparatively insignificant part which the state plays in sound national development, there are special reasons why it looms so large in the eyes of the Western nations. The most important of these is the abnormal growth of industrialism. Normally industrial and commercial expansion is antagonistic to the military spirit and favours peace and the virtues it fosters. But the abnormal industrial and commercial development of the West has reversed this relation. The relation of modern industrialism to militarism is that of allies, not of enemies. From the industrial applications of the Physical Sciences, there have resulted titanic mills and factories but a very small fraction of the produce of which can be absorbed by Europe. Markets outside Europe must, therefore, be found for it, and markets in Western vocabulary have come to mean dependencies and "spheres of influence." The scramble for such markets in Asia and Africa, have made international jealousies and rivalries in the Occident keener than ever before, and is unquestionably the most potent cause of the inordinate militarism of modern Europe. This militarism has necessarily made the State so influential as to usurp functions which should be normally left to the people to discharge. This overwhelming influence of the regulative agency over the regulated part of the community is gradually making the self-government of the latter a nullity, and however beneficial it may appear to be temporarily, spells ultimate ruin to the nation as a whole. My Neo-Indian compatriots without probing the special causes which have made the State so supreme in the West, and without considering the deleterious and paralysing tendencies* of the absorption by the state of activities which should normally be exercised by the people, follow the Western crowd and attach a degree of importance to state agency and to politics which is crushing their manhood and is fraught with the gravest peril to their civilization. This is all the more regrettable as old India enjoyed a measure of real self-government which is not to be met with even among the most advanced nations of

* The following extract from the *New Era* (Nov. 1913) illustrates one aspect of the evil tendencies of a paternal system of Government :—

"No other country in the world has gone so far in paternalism as New Zealand. In no other place has the spirit of regulating every man's business been more zealously fostered. The New Zealand "plan" has for several years been flouted in the face of an older world as the very last word in government.

But, alas and alack ! That paradise of paternalism is right now in the grip of a universal strike. The labouring man has discovered that his troubles are as great as ever, and the business man knows to his dearly-purchased sorrow that there are ills which no amount of specious Government coddling can cure.

While bluejackets from British warships strive to quell the nation-wide rioting, hunger and distress afflict the land. Here we see the actual result of a real application of the socialistic principles of Government.

Such a lamentable failure of the theory that a Government should do everything and attend to every man's business is an object lesson for all mankind. It is a solid pound of fact which outweighs 10,000 tons of fine-spun theories ; the human race cannot be relieved of all its ills by legislation."

the West. "Singular," as says Carlyle, "in the case of human swarms, with what perfection of unanimity and quasi-religious conviction the stupidest absurdities can be received as axioms of Euclid, nay, as articles of faith which you are not only to believe, unless malignantly insane, but are (if you have any honour or morality) to push into practice, and without delay see done, if your soul would live !"

The village community system fostered self-reliance and maintained social order. The communities managed their own affairs relating to education, sanitation, public works, police, law &c., in a way which was well suited to their material condition. If new India instead of pursuing the chimera of Western civilization in cities, remained contented with the simple life and the simple joys of the village, and endeavoured to maintain the simple system of indigenous self-government, the social crisis with which India is threatened to-day might have been averted. The pursuit of the Western path of politics has been an important contributory cause of the increasing invertebracy of the average Neo-Indian. He can hardly stir a step in matters relating to sanitation, education, industry and, sometimes, even to social reform, without invoking the help and initiative of the government. Treated as a child, he remains more or less as such throughout life. He bitterly complains of bureaucratic interference, but acts so as to make such interference inevitable. He talks glibly of self-government, but acts so as to gradually render himself more and more unfit for it. He frequently indulges in platitudes about national progress, but is oblivious of the elementary principles of such progress, that a nation has to work out its own salvation by its own effort, and that the more help it takes from the state beyond a certain limit, the more helpless it becomes.

That there are high-souled, self-sacrificing, men of great parts among my political compatriots is unquestionable, and that they are doing a certain amount of good is also indubitable. But, the good to our mind is outweighed by the evil they have done in undermining the foundations of our cultural swaraj which made our people as happy as it is possible to be in this world for untold generations. In striving for a highly problematical political swaraj of doubtful beneficence, they have, we are inclined to think, sacrificed substance to shadow, the certain to the uncertain.

II

The difficulties in the way of the revival of our Cultural Swaraj are by no means confined to the political sphere as the following examples from my own experience will show. Non-political difficulties.

An esteemed friend of mine with nationalist tendencies took me to task sometime ago for so strongly animadverting upon the pernicious results of pro-Western bias in my "Illusions of New India." He told me that what I have said might have held two or three decades ago, but does not do so now. Then, apparently to confirm his statement, he took me round his drawing room and showed me the paintings with which it is decorated. They are all on Indian subjects and by Indian painters. So far so good, though I may say parenthetically, that they were in close juxtaposition to knick knacks, brica-brac, curtains *etc*, for most of which there is hardly any justification except that they are found in European households. After a time, our conversation fell upon a common friend who had built a fine house in the most fashionable quarter of the town he was living in—a quarter which is almost exclusively occupied by high-placed Europeans. But, my friend observed, what a horrid spectacle does the house present with *saris* drying on the railing of the terrace above the portico. This is a distinctive feature of houses occupied by Indian families who have not yet been completely Westernised. It is certainly offensive to the Western eye, but there is absolutely no reason why it should be so to the Indian. The practice on hygienic, economic and other grounds, is commendable rather than condemnable. And when my friend expressed his abhorrence of it, his judgment, however unconsciously, was warped by Western bias, the result of his Western education and environment.

A friend of mine was complaining to me sometime ago of the extortionate price he had to pay for the socks and shoes of a child of his. I suggested, that in a climate like ours they might be dispensed with to a great extent, if not altogether, without prejudicing the child's health and with decided advantage to his purse. He rejoined : "Must not our æsthetic sense be developed?" It is forgotten that æsthetic development, beyond a certain stage, is more or less a matter of fashion. The sense of the beautiful is innate in man and many other animals. The way in which the peacock displays his gorgeous plumage shows that he and his female companions are aware of its beauty. Savages decorate themselves with ornaments even before they take to clothing. Some of the artistic productions of palæolithic man would not suffer by comparison with those of the present day. But the direction in which the innate æsthetic sense of man is developed is determined by the fashion prevalent in the society in which he lives. The jewellery which gratifies the æsthetic sense of a young lady of old India would usually appear hideous to a young lady of Europe and even of new India. The Indian vocalist of the old type whose "Kalwati" songs enrapture an auditory of old India would be held little short of a nuisance in Europe and in new India.

The æsthetics of drapery after Western fashion referred to by my friend has been gradually developed to such an extent in new India, that it has become one of the most engrossing duties of the parents of a Neo-Indian household, especially of mothers, to deck themselves and their children and even servants as nicely as, and often, I am afraid, more nicely than their means would permit ; and that even in the grilling heat of summer, one, who is not prepared to be taken for a barbarian or a Bedlamite, cannot divest himself of his sartorial impedimenta and sit and work in his house, or enjoy an afternoon siesta, or a walk in the cool of the evening.

There are some observations of Herbert Spencer on this subject of æsthetics which are so apposite, that I can not forbear from quoting them :

"There is one pursuit which nearly all suppose may be carried on without limit—the pursuit of beauty or rather, the pursuit of prettiness. Women particularly, by the daily expenditure of their time, imply the belief that the chief business of life is to please the eye. From the American lady whose idea seems to be, men must work that women may dress, down to the British kitchen-maids whose pleasure during the week is in the thought of vying with her mistress on Sunday, the ambition which goes before all others is to satisfy the æsthetic want ; or rather, to obtain the admiration which is a concomitant, or expected concomitant. * * * If even bones are bent in the effort to obtain admiration, it is inevitable that there will be a moulding of conduct in all ways with the like aim. Appearance will tend ever to become a primary end and use a secondary end ; as with the savage who struts about in a mantle in fine weather, but takes it off when it rains.

As already said, it is not these immediate results, but the remoter results to which attention needs directing. I do not refer only to such remoter results as the injuries to health caused by making dress a thing to look pretty in rather than a thing to be warm in.........but I refer to the ways in which this making of appearance an end supreme over other ends, affects the house at large and the course of domestic affairs. The cottage wife whose small window is so choked with flowers that little light comes in, is not likely, to understand the consequent evils if they are pointed out ; but the lady to whom you explain that light is an important factor in the maintenance of health—so important that patients on the southern side of a hospital recover faster than those on the northern side—and that therefore the sitting in darkened rooms is detrimental, proves no more amenable to reasoning. The welfare of the carpet is an end she thinks more important than the extra health to her family. That the polished floor bordering the carpet often carries mischiefs—bruises, sprains, dislocations—and that even when no such mischief results there is the perpetual fear that prompts careful stepping, are not reasons sufficient to counterbalance in her mind the reason that the polished floor looks well. With the furniture too it is the same. The choice has obviously been determined mainly by the thought of appearance and very little by the thought of comfort. So with the numerous pretty things, or things supposed to be pretty, which burden the tables, the minor pieces of furniture, the brackets, and so on, including such absurdities as paper knives with fret-work handles. The pleasure derived from them, whether by owner or guest, is practically nominal ; there is little beyond the consciousness, that there are pretty things all about. Meanwhile, leaving out the question of original cost they are, in their multitude, constant sources of vexation. The doings of careless housemaids entail disturbances of temper which form a large set-off to any gratifications yielded. Not only, to carry out Bacon's conception, does a man who marries give hostages to fortune, but also he who accumulates objects of value ; for each affords occasions for Fortune's malice."

There is a club for Indians in the town I am living in. It is an excellent institution in its way and serves an useful social purpose. It boasts of a billiard table which is something of the nature of a white elephant, and periodically exercises the brains of the club committee to make it self-supporting. A suggestion for its aboliton, however, does not find a single supporter. The president of the club exclaims: "If the billiard table is done away with, what have we to show the public?" At bottom, the reason for its maintenance is the fact that it forms an almost invariable adjunct of an European club.

There are various sporting clubs among school boys in our town. They send the hat round for subscriptions and donations which one seldom has the heart to refuse. On the last occasion, however, I had the hardihood to smother my feelings and held the following conversation with the boy who came round on such an errand.

Q. Do you know of any indigenous outdoor games which without entailing any expense give as good exercise and afford as much amusement as tennis, cricket, football &c. ?

A. I have heard of such games, but never played any.

Q. Are you aware that a large number of your fellow students are too poor to afford sufficient nourishing food?

A. That is true.

Q. Are not then the costly sports of richer communities a luxury to us?

A. They are.

Q. Is it consistent with one's self-respect that he should beg for luxuries ? and might not the money spent upon them be more advantageously devoted to wholesome nourishing food?

A. It might.

Q. Why do you not then take to the inexpensive native out-door games?

A. Because they have gone out of fashion, and European sports are encourged by the heads of our schools.

The heads being Europeans or Europeanised Indians naturally encourage the sports they have been used to. I told the boy, that if he and his associates went in for Indian games, I would be very pleased to give them a good feed. I do not know whether he took this as a joke. Anyhow, this was more than a year ago, and I have not yet heard that any party of schoolboys has gone back to native games as yet in this town.

On revisiting my native village in Bengal after some years, I was struck by the advance it had made in "civilization" though it was being depopulated by malaria. One of the things that indicated it was a Refreshment room with a prominent signboard in the Bazar which proclaimed to the public, that such delectable refreshments as tea, chops and cutlets were available there. A resident friend who accompanied me informed me, that our villages had been making remarkable "progress," that I would get any quantity of chops and cutlets, but that I would have to search the bazar closely for such a primitive comestible as Muri (puffed rice). These chops and cutlets which are so freely partaken of now-a-days, like the famous sausages of Europe and America, are prepared out of nobody knows what sort of meat and cooked with nobody knows what sort of ingredient. The supersession of such articles as *Muri*, *Chira* (parched rice) cocoanut kernel, *Khoi*, (a preparation of rice) various preparations of gram, *Chhana* (curdled milk), or *Sandesh* (a preparation of chhana) &c. by bread biscuits, pastry, chops, cutlets &c, has been a change decidedly for the worse, at least, for the great majority of our middle class gentry.

The former are quite as palatable as the latter, and quite as nutritious, and have the great advantage of being cheaper and not lending themselves to adulteration. To be wholesome, chops, cutlets, pastry &c. would be far too expensive for the majority of our people. Even in railway refreshment rooms where the charges are very high, the meals supplied are often far from wholesome. I have but little doubt that they would be positively dangerous in the cheap refreshment rooms where the charges are much lower.

In India, at least since the Vedic period, our upper classes have been total abstainers. In the earlier years of English education, indulgence in alcoholic drinks was regarded in Neo-Indian society as a sign of enlightenment and progress. Happily, it is no longer so considered, but the idea has not died out, altogether. The drink evil among the upper classes, however, is confined within a small section. But tea being cheap and exhilarating is becoming a very popular beverage among all classes, among the rich as well as the poor, among men and women, and even among children. It is doing incalculable mischief, especially as Indian tea is generally strong, and its mode of preparation is such as to extract all its strength, it being boiled in many households and the red decoction taken with great gusto. Dyspepsia is the root cause of various ailments, and, I am fully persuaded that in many cases, one of its main causes is the habit of drinking strong tea. In England the popularisation of tea has done some good, as it has weaned many from the much more pernicious habit of indulgence in alcoholic liquors. There tea is a counter-attraction to the much more baneful alcohol. In this country, it is taking the place of the innocent water and *sharbat*. Yet, if I suggest the abolition of tea, I meet with a storm of opposition, the sole argument advanced being, "Do not the Englishmen drink tea and keep good health?" If, perchance, any one should be convinced of the evils of tea drinking, he would at least have cocoa. Some sort of "civilized" drink he must have.

I could multiply instances almost *ad infinitum* to show how the fashion for Western things has gained ground in New India. Herbert spencer talking of Fashion in England says:

> "By and by, however, Fashion......almost wholly ceases to be an imitation of the best, and becomes an imitation of quite other than the best. As those who take orders are not those having a special fitness for the priestly office, but those who hope to get livings; as legislators and public functionaries do not become such by virtue of their political insight and power to rule, but by virtue of birth, acreage and class influence, so, the self-elected clique who set the fashion, do this, not by force of nature, by intellect, by higher worth or better taste, but solely by unchecked assumption. Among the initiated are to be found neither the noblest in rank, the

chief in power, the best cultured, the most refined, nor those of greatest genius, wit, or beauty; and their reunions, so far from being superior to others, are noted for their inanity. Yet, by the example of these sham great, and not by that of the truly great, does society at large now regulate its habits, its dress, its small usages. As a natural consequence these have generally little of that suitableness which the theory of fashion implies should have. Instead of a progress towards greater elegance and convenience, which might be expected to occur did people copy the ways of the really best, or follow their own ideas of propriety, we have a reign of mere whim, of unreason, of change for the sake of change, wanton oscillations from either extreme to the other. And so life *a la mode*, instead of being life conducted in the most rational manner, is life regulated by spendthrifts and idlers, milliners and tailors, dandies and silly women."*

The people who are usually considered "great" by the Neo-Indian community are primarily Europeans, and secondarily high placed Europeanised Indians. Consequently they are imitated in almost all matters pertaining to æsthetics, apparel, diet, games amusements &c.

In the controversy between the Anglicists and the Orientalists in the thirties of the last century, one of the most telling arguments urged by the former in favour of English education was, that it would popularise modern science among the Indian public. It is apprehended by some that the revival of Indian culture would be a set-back to the realization

---

* Spencer's "Essays—Manners and Fashion".

of this highly cemmendable object. The best answer to this objection is, that the institutions which are seeking to revive Indian culture always include modern science in their curricula. Besides, popularisation of science is likely to do more harm than good unless it is based upon the Indian foundation of inherited experience, thoughts, sentiments and ideals. For instance, Sir Charles Bedford in his "Elementary Hygiene for India," which is intended for Indian students and which has run through many editions, says that "the whole body should be washed with warm water and soap once a day ; and the feet, face, and hands oftner. .....Cold baths. are too severe for most people in India." Indian experience for countless generations runs counter to this advice. "Most people in India," not only do not find cold baths "too severe," but find them to be very grateful and beneficial to health. Students who follow Sir Charles Bedford's advice would ruin rather than improve their health. "The teeth", says Sir Charles, "should be brushed at least twice a day with a tooth brush rubbed on a piece of soap." The indigenous practice of brushing teeth with the twigs of Nim and other trees is much more hygienic. In this connection I may quote the following wise words of Herbert Spencer : "Any one variety of creatures in course of many generations acquires a certain constitutional adaptation with particular form of life, and every other variety similarly acquires its own special adaptation. The consequence of that is, if you mix the constitutions of two widely divergent varieties which have severally become adapted to widely divergent modes of life you get a constitution which is adapted to the mode of life of neither, a constitution which will not work properly because it is not fitted for any set of conditions whatever."

Sir Charles Bedford is an Englishman, and may not be reasonably expected to be well acquainted with Indian conditions. I have, however, before me a Bengali Textbook on Hygiene and Domestic Economy (standards III and IV, 1915) by Dr. C. Banks and Dr. Haridhone Dutt (a Bengali). On pages 2 and 3 they say that generally the purpose of cold bath is served by coming out immediately after a plunge, that if the skin assumes its normal glow after it, then it is not injurious, and that if there be a cold sensation after it, then bathing in warm water is healthier etc. If one were to follow this advice, he would have to bid adieu to the pleasures of bathing and swimming, and ultimately abandon the practice of bathing in cold water, for the much less healthy practice, in a climate like ours, of bathing in warm water. I do not know if it is possible for even adults and elderly people to judge of the exact tint of the skin, or of the degree of cold sensation after bath which should regulate its duration or temperature. My school days were passed in a town which is situated on a river. We used to bathe in it every day throughout the year. Happily health primers were not in fashion in our time. Or else good many of us would have had to forego the delights and benefits of a good plunge and swim, and would probably have become hypochondriacs or valetudinarians like so many of the present generation.

On p. I, the authors mention soap as if it were the only means of cleaning the body. The primer is written for Bengali pupils, and one of the authors is a Bengali. Now, in Bengal, it has been a long-established practice to anoint the body with oil before bathing, and rub it out while bathing. The body thus rubbed is fairly well cleaned. I am not in a position to say whether it is cleaned as effectively in this way as by the use of soap. But oil-rubbing invigorates and smooths the body, and, besides, is cheaper, which is an important consideration in a poor community like ours. These advantages so far out-weigh its possible inferiority as a cleanser as to turn the scale in its favour. Besides, "*Besan*" (grampowder) and clay have long been in use in this country as cleansers, and they are I believe, decidedly superior to the class of soaps which could be used by the multitude in this country. In any case, the mention of soap in a way which would lead one to infer its being the only cleansing agent in a primer for Bengali boys and girls, is an instance of dogmatism which can be accounted for only by purblind bias for Western hygiene.

On p. 8, the authors enjoin a change of clothes whenever they get wet with perspiration. I am not sure if such change is absolutely necessary. But even if it were, it would impoverish our poorer middle class to such an extent, that they would not have the means for the food that is indispensable for the maintenance of vitality. And it is decidedly better that one should restrict his sartorial requirements, and run the remote risk of a possible chill than go without nourishing food. Of the two evils, inadequate nourishment is certainly more serious than inadequate habiliment in a climate where one is liable to perspire. In fact, in a climate like that of Bengal, it is doubtful whether the latter is an evil at all.

It did not need a couple of distinguished doctors to give vent to such inanities as—

"ভারতবর্ষের মত উষ্ণপ্রধান দেশে প্রত্যহ সমুদায় দেহ জলে ধৌত করা উচিত" ; "শীতকালে রাত্রে লেপ বা কম্বল দ্বারা দেহ আচ্ছাদিত রাখিবে, নতুবা ঠাণ্ডা লাগিয়া পীড়া হইবার সম্ভাবনা" ; "আমাদের বস্ত্রাদি রীতিমত ধৌত করিয়া ও বাতাসে শুকাইয়া না

লইলে তাহাতে নিশ্চয়ই দুর্গন্ধ হয়;" "তক্তপোস খাট বা কোন উচ্চ শয্যায় শয়ন করা সর্ব্বতোভাবে বিধেয়;" "পান ভোজনাদির বাসনগুলি প্রত্যহ ভাল করিয়া মাজিবে;" রাঁধিবার পূর্ব্বে তরকারিগুলি পরিষ্কার জলে ভাল করিয়া কচলাইয়া ধুইয়া লইবে।"

" In a hot climate like that of India one should have a daily bath." "During winter one should use a quilt or blanket, or else he may catch a cold." " Unless our clothes are washed and dried, they would be sure to have an offensive smell." " It is highly desirable to sleep on bedsteads." " Utensils used for eating and drinking should be washed every day." "Vegetables should be washed in clean water before they are used for cooking."

There is another Bengali Health Primer in the form of a dialogue between a king and a physician in which the latter sings the virtues of tea and coffee in the most glowing terms:

"পরমেশ্বর মনুষ্যের জন্য চা ও কফিনামক দুইটি উত্তম পদার্থ সৃষ্টি করিয়াছেন।..............................ইহা আত্মাকে শান্তি দেয়; চিত্তকে একাগ্র করে; অসুখ দূর করে, ক্লান্তি নাশ করে; বিচারশক্তি বৃদ্ধি করে; শরীরের বল বৃদ্ধি ও নূতন করে এবং বুদ্ধিবৃত্তির সহায়তা করে"।

" God has created two excellent things for man—tea and coffee.................They give peace to the soul, produce concentration, drive away illness, destroy fatigue, favours the growth of the faculty of reason, strengthens and rejuvenates the body ,and helps the development of intellect."

Publications like these serve to drain the tiny purses of our poor people to fill the capacious ones of school-book writers, of tea planters, of publishers, and of printers and paper-manufacturers, but they are not at all likely to check the ravages of disease. On the contrary, as they stuff the impressionable and immature brains of young people with numbers of noxious half truths and falsehoods, and strain them to no useful purpose, they are more likely to injure than to ameliorate health.

III

Aggressive attitude of Neo-Indian Reformers towards Old India.

From what has been said above it will be seen, that the revival of Cultural Swaraj depends largely upon that of Indian culture. We shall see in the next chapter that strenuous efforts are being made in that direction. But the attitude of the most vocal and influential, though numerically the smallest, party is still more or less hostile to it. How grievously poor is the idea of Indian culture entertained by the majority of its leaders will be seen from the following extract from the speech of the Chairman of the

Reception Committee at the last (1928) Session of the Indian National Congress :

"The entire social fabric requires a thorough overhauling, and has to be revolutionised; no amount of tinkering or superimposition of piecemeal reforms would serve our purpose. A frontal attack should be led on the forces of reaction. If it is found that Hindu culture means purdah, and Mahomedan culture means the harem, both must go. If Hindu culture means caste-system and marriage before puberty, and Mahomedan culture means polygamy, none of them should have a place in our social polity. Mere mutual toleration for Hindu and Mahomedan culture is not enough. It is at best a negative virtue; something positive must be done, and the shackles alike of the Shariats and the Shastras should be unceremoniously cast off if they are found to stand in the way of the formation of a united nation."

We are not in favour of any shackles. But as the mass of the people must have them, the indigenous ones are preferable to the exotic. There are some, like the late Lala Rajpat Rai, whose indifference to or contempt for Indian culture is veiled under a desire to combine the best in the Indian and the Western cultures.

Lala Lajpat Rai eloquently exhorted his audience at a meeting of the Indian National

Congress held in Calcutta in 1920 not to be "a copy of the ancient Indians; they wanted to be modern, up-to-date, progressive Indians including all that was best in their culture and in Western culture. They should not go backward, they should go forward. If they hope to carry the world with them, that was only possible by combining the best in the two cultures. Western culture had with all its crookedness done wonders for the world, and they must acknowledge that."

This idea of synthesis is so often, so authoritatively and so insistently repeated in New India, that it would be well to examine it a little closely. There are certain aspects of human nature which are common to mankind all over the globe. As Shylock observed, "hath not a Jew eyes? hath not a Jew hands, organs, dimensions, senses, affections, passions? fed with the same food, hurt with the same weapons, subject to the same diseases, healed by the same means, warmed and cooled by the same winter and summer, as a Christian is? If you prick us do we not bleed? if you tickle us, do we not laugh? if you poison us do we not die? and if you wrong us shall we not revenge? If we are like you in the rest, we will resemble you in that." Then again as I have shown elsewhere,* physical causes have produced

* "Epochs of Civilization."

certain special traits of character among the Europeans and the Indians. But, until the recent Industrial Revolution in Europe due to the unlimited application of science to industry, all that was best in European culture was in accord with all that is best in Indian culture. In fact, the former was to a large extent indebted to the latter. Even now there is a plane of contact in which cultured Westerners, who have not been influenced by modern Industrialism, meet cultured Indians. Culturally, there is hardly any difference between a Romain Rolland and a Rabindra Nath Tagore. It is since the Industrial Revolution that "wanting more wants" has become the basic principle of Western culture (or Kultur as it is called in Germany), and it is so very antagonistic to the fundamental principle of Indian culture which inculcates simple life, keeps desire down to the lowest point of animal necessity, and seeks happiness more through the inner than the outer man, that it is as reasonable to expect to combine them effectively as to combine oil and water.

The idea of a synthesis sounds very well, and along with the great majority of my Neo-Indian friends, I have myself been long governed by it. In fact, it has a flavour of liberality and broad-mindedness about it, which commends it to all who have any pretension to liberal culture. But the difficulties in the way of executing it are so enormous—I might almost say insuperable—that I began to doubt sometime ago whether it could be carried out except perhaps to a small and superficial extent which cannot be called synthesis.

Prima facie, synthesis is impossible. It is possible to have a synthetic dye or synthetic food. But is it possible to have a synthetic civilization worth the name, especially in the case of an ancient civilization like that of the Hindus? I have endeavoured to show in my "Epochs of Civilization," that Hindu civilization is a completed structure—whether perfect or not is a different question—and that Western civilization, however imposing and even majestic it may appear to be at present, is not a completed structure. If, for the sake of argument, it be assumed, that there is a good deal in the Western structure which it is desirable to incorporate with ours, the incorporation cannot be compassed without demolishing the latter and building anew. That, however, would be altogether different from what we understand by synthesis. It is possible to adopt Western methods to some extent in the repairs which the Indian structure needs periodically, but it is impossible to adopt Western design, Western style and Western materials in the main body of the structure without disfiguring, if not destroying it altogether.

True, as Lala Rajpat Rai says, Western culture has done wonders for the world. The world has been marching "forward," and that too at an amazingly furious speed during the last three decades. But one may rush "forward" and be landed in an infernal quagmire, as the elephant of the story enticed by the prospect of sovereignty was. From muzzle-loaders to quick-firing and long-range guns and 'tanks' and asphyxiating gases, from sailing vessels to steamships and submarines, aeroplanes and zeppelins, from handlooms and puny furnaces to huge mills and gigantic smelting furnaces is no doubt wonderful "progress" in the literal sense of the term. But its utter failure to secure the happiness of humanity is writ large in every page of recent history. When labour-saving machinery was applied to cotton-industry, the Western prophets predicted a "Calico-Millenium," and proclaimed that the Angel of Peace would descend in a drapery of calico. The result has been just the reverse—a result which might have been foreseen by any sage nourished upon ancient culture. Instead of the Angel of Peace, there has descended the Demon of War. When quick-firing and long-range guns and other diabolical means of rapid destruction were invented, the wiseacres of the West prophesied that war had become too destructive to be risked by any Power. The result again has falsified the prediction. In no period of the history of civilized man was war so wide-spread, and so enthusiastically engaged in by all sections of the community as it has been of late.

But the vision of the Western and the Westernised people is so be-dimmed by the glamour of modern civilization, that they cannot see its failure, and such their credulity and infatuation, that they would still go on believing in the gospel of modern progress, and repeating its shibboleths and platitudes. And the aspiration of our Westernised reformers is to revolutionise Indian society and bring it into line with the Western.

Not a few of them imagine that if they did that, India would be as powerful and prosperous as England. Then, again, the influence of suggestion is very subtle and very great. There is a story, that a Brahmin once bought a black kid for some Puja which he was carrying on his shoulders to his village. Some of his neighbours wanting to play a practical joke on him divided themselves into several parties, and posting themselves at diverse points on the way the Brahmin was to follow, told him that what he was carrying was not a black kid but a black dog. The first party he poopoohed as blind jackanapes. When, however, the second party said the same thing, he began to doubt whether he had not been imposed upon by the vendor of the supposed kid. But when the third party made the same assertion, he was convinced that what he was carrying was really a dog and not a kid, and threw it down. The calumniation of Indian civilization by writers like William Archer* and Miss Mayo influeuce good many of my Neo-Indian compatriots to jettison it and reform Indian society on the Western model.

That our society like every other society, however civilised, has its evils goes without saying, and we shall, in the next chapter, see the attempts which are being made on Indian lines to remove them. But, on the whole, they are not so serious as those of Western society. This is shown by the statistics of crime. The late W. W. Hunter, who was at the time Director-General of Statistics to the Government of India, observed in 1882 :

"There was now only about one third of the crime in Bengal that there was in England. While for each million

* Says William Archer: "Barbarian, barbarous,—I am sorry to harp so much on these words. But they express the essence of the situation .... There are of course many thousands of individuals who have risen and are rising above it (barbarism), but the plain truth concerning the mass of the Indian population—and not the poorer classes alone—is that they are not civilized people."

persons in England and Wales there were 870 criminals, in Bengal, where the Police was very completely organised, there were 300 convicts in jail for each million; and while in England and Wales there were 340 women in jail in each million of the female population, in Bengal there were less than 20 women in jail for each million of the female population."

In spite of the phenomenal spread of education in England, crime has been increasing apace at a greater rate than the increase of the population. A. Russel Wallace thus summarises the criminal statistics for the thirty years from 1860 to 1889 :—

Years		Prison Population		In Reformatories and Industrial schools		Total
1860—68	...	127,690	...	6,834	...	134,524
1870—79	...	154,154	...	17,394	...	171,539
1880—89	...	170,827	...	25,505	...	196,332

"Here we have," observes Dr. Wallace, "an increase in the average of the first and last ten-year periods amounting to 46 per cent. while the increase of population in the twenty years from 1865 to 1885 is a little less than 30 per cent."*

In the introduction to a Blue-book upon statistics relating to crime in 1909, Mr. H. B. Simpson of the Home Office says :

"The high figure for crime which was a marked feature in the statistics of 1908 is again apparent in the 1909 figures. In 1908, the total number of persons tried for indictable

* The *Wonderful Century*, p. 362.

offences was 68,116, a larger number than in any previous year for which figures are available. In 1909, though not so large as in 1908, it was 67,149, which is considerably larger than in any year before 1908. For the five years 1894—98, the annual average was 52,208; for 1899—1903, it was 55,018; for 1904—08, it was 62,000; and for 1909 it was 67,149."*

In the "Statesman," March 21, 1926, it is stated that "there are sixteen murders in New York for every one in London, and the population is about the same.........Chicago has a population of three millions, and in the year 1925 no less than 373 of its citizens were killed by gunmen. Great Britain has a population of forty millions and only about a hundred murders a year."

Untouchability is unquestionably the worst of Indian social evils and we shall hereafter see the efforts which are being made for its removal. But no "untouchable" could ever have been treated in the outrageously inhuman way

---

* In regard to the Middlesex sessions, Mr. Montague Sharp says :

" It was mentioned to him recently that it is an extraordinary thing that many educated men were being convicted of these offences. He had looked through the calendars from February, 1910 to November, 1911, and he found that out of 200 cases of house-breaking and burglary no less than 83 per cent. were men who were classified as of good education, ...whereas, in regard to larceny, out of 250 cases 69 per cent. were of the third and fourth classes of education. Therefore it was shown that men engaged in nefarious crimes were not of the illiterate class—the old Bill Sikes character—but were men who were certainly educated, and many of whom had received their education at the expense of the community."

in which some Negroes are treated in the United States. It is downright hypocrisy and blatant self-glorification on the part of the Westerners to cry down untouchability as an exceptionally heinous evil of Indian Society.

In the united States of America, "Sixty-five persons (including one woman) were lynched during 1920. Of the victims, thirty one were hanged, fifteen shot, thirteen burned alive, two drowned, one flogged to death, and eight (?) done to death in some unknown manner......It should be remembered that the cold-blooded murder of upward of thirty Negroes in the election riots at Ococe, (Florida) whose only offence was that they had the temerity to approach the polling booth to cast their ballots during the elections last year is not included in the above figures."

The following example will show the horrible way in which lynching is sometimes done :

"The victim (a Negro named Henry Lowery) was chained to a log and then burned alive. More than five hundred persons stood by and looked on while the Negro was slowly burning to crisp. A few women were scattered among the crowd of Arkansas planters, who directed the gruesome work...... ...With the Negro chained to a log, members of the mob, placed a small pile of leaves around his feet. Gasoline was then poured on the leaves, and the carrying out of the death sentence was under the way. Inch by inch the Negro was fairly cooked to death. Every few minutes fresh leaves were tossed on the funeral pyre until the blaze had passed the Negro's waist. As the flames were eating away his abdomen, a member of the mob stepped forward and saturated the body with gasoline........ Once or twice he (Lowery) attempted to pick up the hot ashes and thrust them into his mouth to hasten his death. Each time the ashes were kicked out of his reach by a member of the mob."

Divorce in the United States has increased at such a rate that one out of every seven or eight couples who marry seek this way of release. The evil has gone so far that a philanthropic American has donated £ 250,000 to found a women's college in New York to train women in womanliness and so save their chances of matrimony from being ruined by the system of education in vogue now.

Mr. Price Collier who lived in Germany for some years observes in his "Germany and the Germans" (1913) :

"The period of twenty five years during which I have known Germany has developed before my eyes the concomitants of vast and rapid industrial and commercial progress; and they are: a love of luxury, a great increase in gambling, a materialistic tone of mind, a wide-spread increase of immorality, and a tendency to send culture to the mint and to the market place to be stamped, so that it may be readily exchanged for the means of soft living." In regard to the spread of sexual immorality he speaks of the "monstrous percentage of illegitimacy in Berlin, 20 per cent, or one child out of every five, born out of wedlock; 14 per cent. in Bavaria; and 10 per cent, for the whole empire."

The general moral condition of the Western world is thus painted by Marie Corelli:

"The blight is over all. The blight of atheism, infidelity, callousness, and indifference to honourable, principle—the blight of moral cowardice, self-indulgence, vanity, and want of heart. Without mincing matters, it can be fairly stated, that the aristocratic Jezebel is the fashionable woman of the hour, while the men vie with one another as to who shall best screen her from her amours with themselves. And so far as the sterner sex is concerned the moneyed man is the one most sought after, most tolerated, most appreciated and flattered in that swarm of drones called "society," where each buzzing insect tries to sting the other, or crawl over it in such wise as to be the first to steal whatever honey may be within reach." *

Speaking of present day young women, Sir Arbuthnot Lane, the well-known consulting Surgeon, says:

"The primary factor in the development of cancer is the degeneration of woman in civilization. The poor badly nourished thing has lost most of the normal physical characters which are such marked features in the magnificently built savage. Her capacity to bear and produce children has become complicated by much trouble and innumerable sequelae which too often make life miserable. She is degenerating also in size so that the vast majority of women are puny and insignificant. *Their brains are over-stimulated by what is called education*, by unsuitable foods, and by drugs while the mortgage entailed by their sex makes an abnormally heavy demand upon them. In consequence, they are unable to produce sufficient nourishment and are obliged to fall back upon the deleterious combinations provided for them by food chemists. Their unfortunate children deprived of suitable food, become constipated and their tissues are devitalised by poisons absorbed from their intestines."

"The saintly, self-sacrificing woman," says Bertrand Russell, "belongs to the same order of ideas as the faithful servant, the loyal subject, and the orthodox son of the Church."

* "Free Opinions freely Expressed" p. 82.

The majority of the reformers of New India heedlessly abandon their moorings in the ancient harbour which had been discovered by their ancestors over two thousand years ago after breasting many a storm, and make frantic efforts to follow in the wake of the intrepid, but as yet inexperienced mariners of the West in quest of the "Happy Isles." They do not reflect where those "Happy Isles" are, what they are like, and whether they are likely to be discovered or not. The more thoughtful among the Westerns themselves are apprehensive of the not unlikely contingency of being "devoured by the waves" before that much coveted consummation.* There have been, and still are thoughtful men in the West who appraise their civilization rightly. Rousseau went so far as to declare that "if he were a chief of an African tribe he would erect on his frontier a gallows, on which he would hang without mercy the first European who should venture to pass into his territory, and the first native who should dare to pass out of it," and Rousseau lived long before the mira-

* "Come, my friends,
'Tis not too late to seek a newer world.
... ...
It may be that the gulfs will wash us down :
It may be we shall touch the Happy Isles,"

Tennyson, *Ulysses,*

culous industrial and armamental developments of the present age.

The Neo-Indian reformers sneer at what they call the "primitive," "vegetative" and "bucolic" life of Old India. The truth, however, appears to us to be, that advance from simplicity to complexity, from homogeneity to heterogeneity is beneficial up to a certain limit which has to be determined by physical, economic and ethical considerations. The great thing is not perpetual advance, not continuous rushing forward called progress, but the establishment of a moving equilibrium between the various forces that make for progress. I have dwelt at length upon this subject in my "Epochs of Civilization" and would refer the curious reader to that work. If the equilibrium be maintained, I see no reason why a comparatively simple organism like Hindu society, which secures the happiness of the people without causing misery to humanity as a whole, should not be preferable to the much more complex and imposing, but unequilibriated and, therefore, less stable Western society, which, if it secures the happiness of its members at all, does so at the sacrifice of that of humanity as a whole.

CHAPTER X.

REVIVAL OF CULTURAL SWARAJ—POSSIBILITIES

I

Cultural Swaraj though decadent still exists.

From what has been said in the preceding chapter it will be seen that we are fully alive to the difficulties of the revival of our Cultural Swaraj. They are, however, infinitely less formidable than those which beset the path of political Swaraj. Anyhow, their removal would depend largely upon our own exertions. Then, again, cultural swaraj, though decadent, still exists and would "bow low before the blast" from the West and let the "legions thunder past," but for the fact that the "legions" are being largely recruited locally by militant Neo-Indian reformers with their shibboleths of "wanting more wants," equality, compulsory education, Communism, * Female

* "The march of events during the last few years has shewn the folly of minimising the importance and danger of Communist activities in India. The leaders of the Communist movement in Europe have repeatedly declared, that the first step in the conversion of the masses of the East to communism is to arouse among them discontent with the prevailing conditions of life....That this policy has been pursued in India with vigour during the last two years is evident from the activities of the Workers and Peasants' Parties, which are manned by communists, and have grown in strength and influence under the able guidance of Communist emissaries from abroad." "India in 1927-28" p. 341

Emancipation, &c. The farther one goes from the pernicious influence of modern civilization with its Law Courts, Railways etc., the more is India's cultural swaraj in evidence, I have mixed with our people intimately away from such influence in rearly all parts of India (including Burma), and I have almost invariably found them healthier* (morally as well as physically) and happier than their civilized brethren. As long ago as 1831, Raja Rammohan Ray observed:

"From a careful survey and observation of the people and inhabitants of various parts of the country, and in every condition of life, I am of opinion, that the peasants or villagers, *who reside at a distance from large towns and head stations and courts of law,* are as innocent, temperate and moral in their conduct

---

* Except in Bengal, where malaria does great havoc in the villages, death rate in rural areas is lower than in the urban. The figures for the whole of British India from 1920 to 1926 are as follows :

Year	Death-rate (Rural)	Death-rate (urban)
1920 ...	30·49	34·65
1921 ...	30·32	33·33
1922 ...	23·00	27·41
1923 ...	24·58	29·27
1924 ...	28·18	31·66
1925 ...	24·27	29·21
1926 ...	26·19	32·52

(" Statistical Abstract for British India," 1928)

as the people of any country whatsoever; and the farther I proceed towards the North and West, the greater the honesty, simplicity, and independence of character I meet with."

The same observation *mutatis mutandis* holds good at the present day. During nearly forty years of touring in the jungles I had not a single case of theft, though the people had abundant opportunities for it. Almost invariably did I find them honest, truthful and straightforward. A European Magistrate of the Khasi Hills told me, that when he had a primitive Khasia clad in homespun loin cloth in his court he believed every word he said; but, when a well-dressed "civilised" Khasia appeared, he was on his guard and prepared to hear a lot of lies. The unsophisticated people also excel in the virtues of benevolence,* charity and hospitality, and scenes like the following described by James Forbes in his "Oriental Memoirs" are by no means unusual :—

"I sometimes frequented places where the natives had never seen an European, and were ignorant of everything concerning us : there I beheld manners and customs simple as were those in the patriarchal age ; there in the very style of Rebecca and the damsels of Mesopotamia, the Hindu villagers treated me with that artless hospitality so delightful in the poems of Homer, and other ancient records. On a sultry day, near a Zinore village, having rode faster than my

* *Vide ante* pp 23—26,

attendants, while waiting their arrival under a tamarind tree a young woman came to the well; I asked for a little water, but neither of us having a drinking vessel, she hastily left me, as I imagined, to bring an earthen cup for the purpose, as I should have polluted a vessel of metal; but as Jael, when Sisera asked for water, "gave him milk, and brought forth butter in a lordly dish,"—Judges, Ch. V; Ver. 25, so did this village damsel with more sincerity than Heber's wife, bring me a pot of milk, and a lump of butter on the delicate leaf of the banana, "the lordly dish" of the Hindus. The former I gladly accepted; on my declining the latter, she immediately made it up into two balls, and gave one to each of the oxen that drew my hackery. Butter is a luxury to these animals, and enables them to bear additionl fatigue."

I have traveresed large areas where there are no police-stations and no Courts of Law, and where one's word is his bond. Health, peace of mind and independence are the three important requisites of happiness, and the primitive rurals have a much larger share of these than the "civilised" urbans. In fact, had not the deep-grained habits of innumerable generations unfitted our Bhadralok class for hard manual labour, it would be a blessing for the majority of them to exchange their lot with the former.

Communal antagonism is but little known away from large towns and cities. Amity still prevails among all sections of our community in the interior—Hindus, Mahomedans, Christians and Aborigines (Mundas, Oraons, Gonds, Bhils etc.). A society has been started in the town I am living in, Ranchi, called the Chota-Nagpore Go-Rakshini and Jati Sudhar Sabha (Chota Nagpore Society for Cow Protection and Reform). It has numerous branch societies affiliated to it and its operations are carried on all over Chota Nagpur which comprises the districts of Ranchi, Hazaribagh, Palamow, Singbhum, and Manbhum. The area being what is known in Indian parlance as "backward" is still pervaded by communal concord, and all sections of the community work together for the society just mentioned in fraternal spirit. And I was agreeably surprised some time ago to find a Mahomedan member so carried away by his enthusiasm for cow-protection as to earnestly preach against cow-killing.

The mass of our people, though illiterate, are generally not such numskulls or sunk in such "ignorance, superstition and squalor" as they are usually supposed to be. Their abodes appear to the Western or Westernised eye as mere hovels, but they are usually clean hovels and are much better than the slums of industrial centres. The homestead is generally kept as clean as their means would permit, and the kitchen and the utensils for cooking and eating are kept scrupulously clean. In personal cleanliness the Hindus are, class for class, more particular than the peoples of the West. In fact, as Elphinstone observed long ago:

"The cleanliness of the Hindus is proverbial." The writer has often noticed that away from large towns where there are streams with sandy beds, the villagers dig holes in the sands, and carefully ladle out the water therefrom for drinking which shows the importance they attach to it.

"The ryots of India," says Sir H. J. S. Cotton, "possess an amount of knowledge and practical skill within their own humble sphere which no expert scientist can ever hope to acquire." "The Indian peasant," observes Sir T. W. Holderness, "though illiterate is not without knowledge. He has been carefully trained from boyhood in the ritual and the religious observances of his forefathers. He hears the ancient epics read in their pithy vernacular form. He is full of lore about crops and soils and birds and beasts."

"The Indian peasant," says Sir H. Risley, "is no fool. He has his limitations like his class all over the world, but within the compass of his own village and its immediate surroundings, he is just as shrewd a person as one could wish to meet." Comparing him with the English rustic of the counties, he (Sir H. Risley) was much inclined to think that "the Indian was the sharper of the two."

Sir Lepel H. Griffin says, "that judged by any truthful standard the people of India were on a far higher level of morality than Englishmen ; that they were industrious, sober, chaste, and religious, that a drunken man was rare, and that a drunken woman was unknown."

Agricultural outlook.

New India is under no illusion as to the material condition of the mass of the people of India. It reverberates with the cry of their excessive poverty, and of their gradual impoverishment in recent times. The condition of our agricultural classes who constitute more than three-fourths of our population is no better, and is probably worse now than in 1878 when Sir James Caird wrote :

"Three-fourths of the cultivators have no capital. In a good year they have enough for their simple wants ; in a year of abundance their banker has something to apply in reduction of their debt ; in an unfavourable year they live very poorly, and partly by help of their credit ; in a year of famine, that is withdrawn, and they have no means left of employing labour, and the poorest of them and their labourers are equally destitute." *

We have already seen how the insensate cry for mass education is weaning the more intelligent and resourceful of our peasantry from their hereditary callings. In pre-British and early British times the majority of the upper classes lived by agriculture which was esteemed as the best of all occupations.† Their intellectual capacity and resourcefulness greatly furthered the extension and developement of

* " India the Land and the People " pp. 212—213.

† This is shown, among other things, by grants of land by indigenous governments for good service and learning, and by various popular Sanskrit slokas, one of which translated runs as follows :—

" One may leave household management in the hands of one who is like his father, the management of the kitchen with one who is like his mother, that of the cattle with one who is like himself, but he must attend to cultivation himself."

agriculture and horticulture. But as a result of various causes, among which the wide extension of the present system of Education is one of the most important, they are abandoning, in annually, increasing numbers the healthy, peaceful, and useful rural life, for the unhealthy restless, and comparatively useless urban life.

The increase of population (which is by no means high), and the decadence of indigenous industry have enormously increased the pressure upon land. But its productive capacity appears to be either stationary or diminishing.

"Wheat land in the North-West Provinces," says Sir W. Hunter, "which now gives only 840 lbs. an acre, yielded 1140 lbs, in the time of Akbar." * The food-grains which are exported in such large quantities are generally supposed to represent the surplus left after meeting the requirements of the country. "It may, however, be alleged with some truth," says the same writer, "that if the whole population ate as much as they could, the surplus would not exist. The grain exports of India represent many hungry stomachs in India... ......If all the poor classes in India ate two full meals every day, the surplus for export would be much less than at present. That surplus only proves that the yearly supply of food in India is greater than the effective demand for it."

---

* *England's Work in India*, pp. 88 & 75-76. It should be observed that no reliable statistics are available concerning the recent deterioration of the soil, and there are authorities who aver that there has been no deterioration at all.

It is true a good deal of land which had either never been cultivated before or had run to waste during the troublous times consequent upon the disruption of the Moghul Empire, has recently been brought under cultivation. But already, "the clearing and cultivation of the jungles have been carried to such an excess in some parts of India as to seriously alter the climate. For forests, and the undergrowth which they foster, not only husband the rainfall, but they appear to attract it." "The pasture grounds of the villages have also, to a large extent, been brought under the plough, and the cattle in many districts have degenerated from insufficient food. The same number of oxen can no longer put the same amount of work into the soil." *

Mr. S. S. Thorburn who made a special study of the condition of the peasantry in the Punjab, says, that "there was no general indebtedness in any village before 1871," But about two decades later, of 474 villages examined by him he found only 138 slightly involved. Of the remainder he found 210 seriously, and 126 hopelessly indebted. The total indebtedness of these three groups of villages was found to amount to about Rs. 19,78,003. Mr. Thorburn's inquiry showed that the common idea that the indebtedness of the peasantry is largely due to their extravagance on marriages is not supported by evidence. In four circles, he found in one the indebtedness due to such extravagance to be only 6½ per cent of the total indebtedness ; in another it was not more than 7 per cent ; in the third 8 per cent ; and in the fourth 11 per cent. "Of 742 families," remarks Mr. Thorburn, "only in 3 cases was marriage extravagance the cause of their serious indebtedness." The growth of indebtedness of the cultivating class in every part of India except Bengal is as formidable as in the the Punjab. During the quinquennium, 1904—1909, the number of land transfers by order of the court increased from 25,153 to 25,722, and by private contract or gift from 556,821 to 1,122,245.

* Hunter, *op cit* pp. 65—66.

In four Deccan districts with an aggregate population of some 4 million souls, Mr, Digby found the Ryots' annual borrowings to have increased from £306,667 in 1885 to £448,667 in 1892. *

Various causes have been assigned for this colossal poverty. The annual drain on account of the Home charges and remittances of the profits from railways and various commercial undertakings, and of the savings of officials and others, which is now computed at over twenty millions sterling, is urged by some as the main cause of India's impoverishment.† There are others who lay stress upon the stringency of the present Land Revenue System, and upon the revision and undue enhancement of assessment at comparatively short intervals.

" In no respect," says Sir H. J. S. Cotton, " are we more ready to contrast British rule with native rule so largely in our own favour as in our dealings with the land. We point to our equitable assessments as enhancing the value of landed property, to our agricultural experiments increasing its productiveness, and to the bengin protection of the British Government as enabling the Ryot and his family to enjoy the fruits of their toil in unmolested quiet. But there is not one of these beliefs which is not delusive. Our dealings with the land have been more destructive of all ancient proprietory rights than were the old methods which preceded our own. Our rigid and revolutionary methods have reduced the peasantry to the lowest extreme of poverty and wretchedness, and the procedure of our settlement courts has been the

---

* "Prosperous India" p. 349.

† *Vide ante* Ch. VI.

means of laying upon them burdens heavier than any they endured in former times. Famine is now more frequent than formerly, and more severe, and it is the irony of fate that our Statute book is swollen with measures of relief in favour of the victims whom our administrative system has impoverished" "Short settlements," says the same writer, "an exacting demand, and an unbending severity in collecting rent have driven the simple husbandmen into the clutches of the money lender, and are responsible for their share in intensifying the effects of famine."*

The success of the recent passive resistance to iniquitous assessment at Bardoli ably engineered by Mr. Vallabhai Patel leads one to hope that Government will revise their Land Revenue system so that in future heavy assessment may not drive the ryot into the clutches of the usurer. On the other hand, the rapid expansion of the Cooperative movement since the beginning of the present century is lightening his load of indebtedness, and is otherwise benefiting him in a variety of ways.† The Agricultural Department has hitherto done him but little good partly because it has not been in touch with him. It is a good augury for the future that the Government Experimental Farms have now begun to work in cooperation with the Cooperative Central Banks which not

* "New India," Revised edition, pp 68—69, 77.

† The number of Cooperative Societies in British India has risen from 24,393 in 1917-18 to 69,016 in 1925-26, that of members from 1,048,290 to 2,877,550, and that of share capital from 2,10,59,574 to 6,71,84,542.

only distribute improved seeds and artificial manures to the rural societies affiliated to them but also try to impart agricultural instruction to the cultivators. They are not so pachydermatous and perversely conservative as they are usuallysupposed to be, and are quite ready to introduce improvements in their cultivation if they are demonstrated to be to their advantage, as is evidenced, among other things, by the recent extension of potato and groundnut cultivation, and of "garden cultivation" where they can afford it, the almost universal adoption of the improved Sugar Mill, etc. The multitudinous varieties of food-grains and fruits, the mechanical contrivances for irrigation etc. show, among other things, that they are not wanting in knowledge or intelligence.

Dr. Voelcker, a renowned agriculturist, who was, some years ago, engaged by the Government to report upon the possible directions in which our agriculture might be improved, says, after carefully inspecting nearly every part of India: "I unhesitatingly dispose of the ideas which have been erroneously entertained that the ryots' cultivation is primitive and backward, and say, that nearly all the attempts made in the past to teach him have failed because he understands far better than his would-be teachers, the particular circumstances under which he has to pursue his calling."

There are other ways in which the Cooperative Movement is benefiting the cultivator. The Aborigines, the Hindus, the Mahomedans and the Christians meet together in many rural societies under a unifying sense of joint responsibility, elect as their President the man whom they consider to be best fitted for the post irrespective of caste and creed, and sometimes carry out beneficent schemes such as construction of *bunds* (for irrigation purposes), wells, roads etc. Then, again, there are some Central Banks which are endeavouring to minimise the evils of litigation by settling by arbitration many cases affecting the members of the societies affiliated to them. Altogether, the Cooperative movement is pregnant with immense possibilities for the future welfare of our peasantry.

Industrial outlook.

As we saw in Chapter VI, the resuscitation of indigenous industry depends upon the harmonious working of the positive and negative methods. For reasons stated there, we are inclined to stress the latter. Its application, however, would depend upon the revival of the principles of Indian culture; and as we shall presently see, earnest efforts are being made in that direction.

Our artisans, like our cultivators, though generally illiterate, readily take to improved appliances, designs etc. if they find these advantageous. As has been observed by the Industries Commission, "it must not be imagined, however, that the artisan of today is uninfluenced by the industrial changes of the past century. His methods remain the same, but in some instances he works with superior raw materials and in others with better tools. The weaver has taken to mill yarn, the dyer to synthetic dyes, the brass and coppersmiths to sheet metal, the blacksmith to iron roll, rolled in convenient sections, in each case with advantage to himself from the lessened cost of production which has greatly extended his market. In some districts in lower Bengal, the weavers use the fly shuttle sley extensively, and they have recently adopted it in large numbers in the coast districts of the Madras Presidency, while it is also gradually coming into use elsewhere. The tailors invariably employ sewing machines, and town artisans readily take to improved tools of European or American manufacture." The Commission observed : "that the cottage industries are a very important feature in the industrial life of India; that they are by no means so primitive as they are usually depicted: that there is no real ground for belief that they are generally in a decadent condition; and that their numbers are still vastly larger than those of the operatives employed in organised industries."

The people in outlying jungles are still clad in homespuns. But the *charka* became practically extinct in New India with the extension of the Railways. In the subject committee of the Industrial Conference held in Calcutta in 1906, a suggestion for its revival was laughed out as too ridiculous for the twentieth century. During the last decade, however earnest efforts have been made for its revival by Mahatma Gandhi, Dr. P. C. Roy and others. Organisations for the promotion of Charka spinning financed by the All India Spinners' Association, have sprung up in various parts of the country; and that considering the formidable difficulties in their way they have made considerable progress is unquestionable. During 1926-27, twenty four lakhs worth of khadi was produced, and over thirty three lakhs worth was sold. Though I whole-heartedly admire the efforts which are being made in this direction, I am sceptical about any large measure of success under existing conditions. Just as muzzle-loading guns would be of not much use in present-day warfare against quick-firing rifles, so, I am afraid, the *charka* alone would not be able to compete with the power-driven spindle. The former, under existing conditions, can supply only an insignificant fraction of the yarn needed for our cloth requirement. It is therefore, a good sign that the number of spindles increased from 6, 170, 990 in 1917-18 to 7, 621, 589 in 1926-27 in Britih India, and from 443, 279 to 791, 228, within the same period in Native States and Foreign Territories. With mill-made yarn, the prospect of the revival of our handloom industry is very hopeful. In 1913-14, India imported 3,198,542,467. yards of piece goods. In 1926-27, however, the imports fell to 1,787,944,368 yards. As the presumption is that our cloth requirement has increased rather than decreased within that period the deficiency of about a billion and a half yards must have been supplied by Indian mills and by handlooms. The Indian mill production has increased by about 800 million yards since 1913-14, so the balance of about 700 million yards has presumably been supplied by hand-looms. We have no reliable statistics to gauge the progrees of the hand-loom industry, but that it is being successfully revived there is not the shadow of a doubt.

As in the case of agriculture, so in that of industry, the Co-operative movement promises to be very helpful. For, instance, a Weavers' Stores started under the auspices of the Ranchi Central Co-operative Bank has been extending the use of improved looms among the weavers and introducing improved designs and the weaving of silk and woollen fabrics. At Bankura and various other pleces also, Co-operative Weavers' Societies have sprung up which are doing very useful work. And it is not unreasonable to hope, that India will regain her cloth autonomy—which is one of the main props of her cultural Swaraj—in the near future, especially if we can adopt the negative method and go back to the textile requirements which obtained two or three generations ago suited to our climate and economic condition.*

II

Social reforms.

If a society is to survive, a certain amount of progress is necessary, but to be benificent order should not be sacrificed to it, at least to any large extent. Hindu civilization attained its highest, the ethical stage over two thousand years ago. As the attainment of the equipoised condition of that stage necessarily reduces mobility to some extent, it has since then been exuberantly encrusted with thick parasitic outgrowths of ignorance and superstition. The function of the reformers of old India from the time of Gautama Buddha down to that of Ramkrisna Paramhamsa has always been to remove these adventitious excrescences and expose the underlying genuine substance, and, unlike the majority of the reformers of New India, they have done this without seriously disturbing the order, and jeopardising the stability of our society.

---

* The Industries Commission of 1916 found, that between two and three million handlooms were then at work in India, the annual gross earnings of which amount to some fifty crores of rupees.

At the present day, such organisations as the Arya Samaj, the Ramkrishna Mission, the Hindu Mahasabha and the Hindu Mission are following in their footsteps. Their yearly increasing activities, especially in relaxing, if not removing, the extreme rigidity of the caste system, * which is the most crying of the social evils among the Hindus, are very hopeful.

Intemperance is the worst of the social evils among our lower classes, especially the aborigines. In the district I am living in (Ranchi), I calculated three years ago that no less than 70 per cent of its Government Revenue is derived from Excise, and that no less than a crore of rupees was wasted upon country spirit by the people of the distillery area. Besides, intemperance is the most potent cause of such heinous crime as there exists in the district. The influence of the great Vaishnava reformer Sri Chaitanya, who passed through these parts is still discernible among a section of the aborigines who calling themselves Bhagats gave up drinking alcoholic liquors. The spiritual temperament of our people makes them highly susceptible to the influence of holy men. By elevating the people in the spiritual and ethical plane they have conferred lasting benefits upon them. But for

---

* *Vide* "Some Present day Susperstitions" Chapter III.

them our cultural Swaraj would not have survived to the present day. I have referred to the recent appearance of one of them among the Gonds of the Rewa State.* In the Ranchi district, another *sadhu* appeared a few years ago, and a considerable section of the Oraons has, in accordance with his injunction, abjured meat and alcoholic drinks. These *sadhus* are not confined to the higher castes. In the early part of the last century, in the district of Raipur (Central Province). Ghasi Das, an unlettered but thoughtful Chamar (one of the lowest of Hindu castes), was deeply impressed by the degraded condition of his community who were strongly addicated to alcoholic drinks and other vicious habits. He gradually acquired considerable influence by his wisdom and high moral character, and gathered round him a handful of devoted followers. One morning he collected them, and telling them to assemble all the Chamars at a particular spot after six months, himself retired behind the hills in the south-eastern portion of the district of Raipur to medidate and hold communion with God. On the appointed day a large concourse of the Chamars was brought together to receive God's message from Ghasi Das. The reformer slowly appeared with the rising sun and gave the

* *Vide ante* p. 25.

message, which among other things proclaimed the unity of the Godhead (Sat Nam) and interdicted meat, intoxicating liquors and smoking. The message was received with great enthusiasm and the Satnami sect was established. Nearly all the Chamars of the districts of Raipur and Bilaspur belong to this sect, and I have nowhere come upon a finer, sturdier set of cultivators. *

As reformers of the type mentioned above are getting rather scarce under modern influences, it is a hopeful augury of the future, that there are springing up organisations like the Chota Nagpur Society for cow-protection and social reform. It has been started at the initiative of the socalled lower, mostly illiterate classes—the Oraons, Mundas, Telis, Kurmis, Kahars &c.—and is mainly piloted by them, the secretary being an Oraon. Besides cow-protection, its objects are the promotion of temperance, settlement of disputes by arbitrators instead of Law courts, and the resuscitation of indigenous industry, that is to say some of the most salient reforms needed for the revival of cultural Swaraj.

It has been in existence for only five years. So it is too early yet to judge of the result

---

* Some of the Chamars gradually found that it was hard work abstaining from smoking as well as drinking and formed themselves into a subsect called *Chungia*.

of its operations. But if it goes on working as vigorously as it has been doing, there can be no doubt that it will achieve a large measure of success. No less than sixty largely attended meetings were held last year in different parts of Ranchi, Manbhum, Palamow, Singbhum and Hazaribagh districts. As a result of the propaganda for cow-protection, breeding bulls have been secured in various places and large numbers of aborigines and others have given up beef. As a tangible result of the movement it is reported that milk is slightly cheaper at places than before. And that is a great gain, considering the fact that the scarcity and dearness of milk is one of the main causes of our recent deterioration of health. Then, in regard to the drink evil which is the greatest curse of Chota Nagpur, there has been considerable abatement of it. The Excise Report of 1924-25, showed a reduction of two thousand gallons in the consumption of country spirit in the Ranchi district, and the latest Report to which I have had access, that for 1926-27, shows a further reduction of no less than 14, 790 gallons. I am strongly inclined to think, that this diminished consumption is mainly attributable to the energatic propaganda carried on by the Chota Nagpur Reform Association. Organisations working on similar lines must be in existence in other parts of the country. But their work, carried on silently and quietly, attracts but little notice in New India, and is seldom reported in its newspapers.

III.

Constructive efforts for revival of Indian Culture.

It is one of the happy signs of the times that in the tug-of-war which, for sometime past, has been going on between Western and Indian culture, the forces on the side of the latter have of late been strengthening. The number of institutions based on the indigenous *Brahmacharya* system of the "Tols" but adapted to modern conditions, and including the modern sciences in their courses of study has been yearly increasing. Probably the most important of these is the Gurukula University near Hardwar, which was established in 1902 chiefly through the self-sacrificing efforts of the late Mahatma Munshi Ram (Swami Sraddhananda). Mr. J. Ramsay Macdonald who visited it some years ago observed that "it is the most momentous thing in Indian education that has been done since Macaulay sat down to put his opinions into minute in 1835." There are about a dozen Gurukulas affiliated to the Gurukula University and they are educating over one thousand boys. A Gurukula for girls with over one hundred pupils has recently been started.

About the same time as the Gurukula was established the Santiniketan Brahmacharya Asram by Dr. Rabindra Nath Tagore which has since developed into a University well known as the Viswabharati. The Brahmacharya Vidyalaya of Ranchi, started in 1917, owes its existence to the exertions of Swami Yogananda Giri and the munificence of Sir Maharaja Manindra Chandra Nandy and educates about 150 pupils. Two schools on the same lines have been recently established near Purulia, and one is about to be started at Gidni in the district of Midnapur. Conferences have been held this year at Ranchi and Calcutta for devising measures for the expansion of the Brahmacharya system of education. The Ramkrishna Mission Vidyapith at Deogarh, the Asram of the Prabartak Sangha at Chandernagore (which was founded in 1915 by Motilal Roy), the Khulna and the Madaripur Brahmacharya Vidyalayas of the Bharat Sevasram Sangha, the Satsang Tapovan near Pabna, the Abhoy Asram of Comilla, and the Rishikula Brahmacharya Asram at Hardwar are some of the more noteworthy institutions imparting education on Brahmacharya lines.

In regard to female education on Brahmacharya principles, besides the Gurukula mentioned above the Nibedita Girl School established by Sister Nibedita of the

Ramkrishna Mission, the Benares School for girls founded by Mrs. Annie Besant, the Saradeswari Asram deserves notice. It was established in 1895 by Mataji Gauripuri Devi at Barrackpore, but has since been removed to Calcutta.

There are also numerous educational organisations, which though they do not strictly follow Brahmacharya principles, have for their object the propagation of Indian culture, such as the Dayananda A. V. College at Lahore, the National Council of Education in Bengal, the Osmania University of Hyderabad (Deccan) the Hindu University of Benares, the Aligarh University, the Poona University for Women, the Vidyapiths at Ahmedabad, Patna, Benares, etc., and the institutions which have been established in different parts of India for reviving Indian Art and the Indian system of Medicine. Then, again, the number of institutions which indirectly spread Indian culture is yearly increasing. Foremost among these are the Maths and Sevasrasmas of the Ramkrishna Mission, numbering over one hundred scattered all over India, Burma, the Federated Malaya states and the United States of America. The Indian centres render invaluable service during floods and other calamities besides ministering to the spiritual wants of our intelligentsia and the temporal wants of the sick and the needy.

The foreign centres at New York, California and San Francisco chiefly spread the principles of the Vedanta philosophy which may be said to be the quintescence of Indian Culture. In this connection the following account of the propagation of Indian culture in America from a recent issuse of the *Statesman* will be found interesting :

"During the past few months I have made several references in this journal to a new form of missionary enterprise that has sprung up in the United States. Ever since the World's Parliament of Religions, which was held in Chicago in 1893, there has been a gradual but well-directed effort made by religious teachers and philosophers to spread a knowledge of Indian religious thought throughout the United States. Several of the best known Western-educated teachers of Hinduism, natives of India, visited the United States for the 1893 Congress, and from that time dates the new missionary work. The progress resulting from at first the sporadic instances of Buddhist (and Moslem) effort at proselytism, and latterly consistent missionary effort, has been considerable in many parts of the country, the result being that to-day one is able to visit Buddhist churches and circles in most of the large cities. Among the visitors to the United States in 1893 there was no more striking figure from Asia than Vivekananda, who did much to create an interest in the Vedanta philosophy. Subsequent to the Congress, it may be recalled, he delivered a series of masterly lectures in New York which attracted widespread attention, his first book, "Raja Yoga," with Patanjali's aphorisms and commentaries, running into many large editions, as have many of his other books dealing with the same subject. This brilliant young scholar—who died in India soon after his return from the United States at a year or two over thirty—may be called the pioneer of Indian thought in America, and though many have followed him not one has succeeded either on the platform or in book form to the same extent. Another outstanding figure in Buddhist circles here is the venerable Bishop Mazzinianananda, who was prominent in San Francisco at the time of the 1915 Exposition and who has established several churches in the Middle West and the Western states.

* * * *

This interesting centenarian, who has the personal appearance of a man of sixty, possesses the mental energy of most men at forty. In 1893 he came for the first time to the United States, where he has lived ever since, and now conducts a Church of Universal Truth at Oakland, California. He has instructed thousands of Americans in the tenets of Buddhism, and is certainly a striking example of his preachments of longevity. If Sri Sumangala, of Ceylon, is not still alive, I believe that I am right in saying that Dr. Mazzinianananda is the oldest active Buddhist monk out of India and Tibet.

In Los Angeles a very considerable following has been built up by Swami Yogananda a Brahmin educated at either Oxford or Cambridge, who literally swept this country by storm in a nation-wide tour some years ago. He followed the set plan of the usual lecturer of giving a few free lectures, subsequently enrolling members to a private class of instruction, at a charge of 25 dollars for the course, and is said to have collected in fees something like a million dollars. He now has a large class of instruction by mail, issues one or two magazines on higher thought lines, and is without doubt doing a great deal of good. New York, Chicago, Philadelphia and many of the other large cities have also been served in somewhat the same way by other Swamis, and it now appears that the time is ripe for the co-ordination of all activities in the field."

India owes a deep debt of gratitude to such European Scholars as Sir William Jones, Colebrooke, Max Muller, Weber &c. for making the treasures of Indian culture available to the civilized world. The number of scholars, Indian as well as foreign, who have been following in their footsteps, has been increasing and gathering round such bodies as the Asiatic Societies of India, England, and other places, the societies for the promotion of vernacular literatures, the Greater India Society etc. The Theosophical Society which was founded in 1875 by Col. Olcott and Madame Blavatsky is inspired by the spiritual teachings of Hinduism. Its activities have been increasing and now extend all over the civilized world. In 1928, it had Lodges in America, Europe, India, Australia etc. aggregating 1,586 with 45,098 members. The attenuation in the number of old fashiond *Maths*, is being amply compensated by the augmentation of that of organisations better adapted to the present environment like the Ramkrishna Mission, the Arya Samaj, the Mahabodhi Society of Calcutta with its branches in London, New York etc. the Bharat Dharma Mahamandal of Benares, the Hindu Mission, the Vedic Mission, the Bharat Sevasram Samgha, the Radhasaomi Satsang, and the Asramas of Arabinda Ghosh at Pondicherry and of Mahatma Gandhi at Subarmati.

Concluding observations.

The forces we have briefly noticed above are as yet too feeble to fight successfully those of Western Civilisation. The future of India —and, I may venture to say, of the whole civilized world—would depend upon whether they will continue to gather strength as they have been doing of late. At present they are isolated, and are but little noticed in the press of New India. The formation of a central organization under some such title as Society for the Promotion of Cultural Swaraj would, I think, add considerably to their strength, solidarity and usefulness. It is the propagation of ancient culture, which is at present best represented by Indian culture, that can rescue humanity from the morass of militarism, malevolence, greed, selfishness, destitution, disease, and vice in which it has of late been sinking more and more deeply. The principles which underlie it—renunciation and universal all-embracing benevolence—are among the eternal verities. They hold good to-day as they did some three to four thousand years ago when they were formulated and preached in India and China. Not that the mass of the people should renounce the world; and it is not desirable that they should do so, but the noble examples of ascetic saints serve as an inspiration to them in observing the discipline of simple living and selflessness in a way which no amount of preaching would do. And without simple life and self abnegation genuine altruism is not possible. The West also preaches altruism, but simultaneously propagates industrialism and the cult of self-indulgence, euphemestically called "elevation of the standard of living," which are utterly antagonistic to it. Natural Science which forms the foundation of modern Western culture has, on its theoretical side, done most commendable work. It has extended the domain of Law in the kingdom of Nature. On its practical side also, in medicine and surgery, and to some extent also in agriculture, its effect has been to alleviate human misery. But the good thus conferred is confined to a comparatively insignificant fraction of humanity and is far outweighed by the evils arising from its endless industrial and military applications. If it had been subordinated to philosophical culture ; if it had not been so extensively employed for saving manual labour and killing cottage industries, for perpetually adding to comforts and luxuries and intensifying the struggle for animal existence, and for improving the engines of destruction ; if, in short, it had not lent its aid so largely to material progress, and had kept more within the bounds of intellectual and ethical culture, we would have unqualified praise for it. But its wonderful practical applications which form such a fertile theme for exuberant encomium in the West arouse in us only feelings of anxiety and apprehension for the stability of Western Civilization. These applications which are generally considered by Western writers as its chief title to commendation are, to our mind, its chief title to condemnation. So long as the present insensate rage for invention continues ; at least, so long as the zeal for it is not tempered by ancient culture, so long there does not appear to be any prospect of peace and prosperity on anything like a durable basis.

Happily, the West is gradually waking up to a sense of the colossal evils of its industrial civilization:

"Even the best of Modern Civilizations," declared Huxley emphatically, "appears to me to exhibit a condition of mankind which neither embodies any ideal, nor even possesses the merit of stability. I do not hesitate to express the opinion that if there is no hope of a large improvement of the condition of the greater part of human family ; if it is true that the increase of knowlodge, the winning of a greater dominion over nature which is its consequence, and the wealth which follows upon that dominion, are to make no difference in the extent and the intensity of want with its concomitant physical and moral degradation amongst the masses of the people, I should hail the advent of some kindly comet which would sweep the whole affair away as a desirable consummation". Referring to the indutsrial perfection of England, Ruskin exclaimed in his usual vigorous language : "Alas, if read rightly these perfectnesses are signs of a slavery in our England a thousand times more bitter and degrading than that of the scourged helot Greek. Men may be beaten, chained, tormented, yoked like cattle, slaughtered like summer flies, and yet remain in one sense, and the best sense, free. But to smother their souls within them, to blight and hew into rotting pollards the sucking branches of their human intelligence, to make the flesh and skin into leathern thongs to yoke machinery with—this is to be slave masters indeed ; and there might be more freedom in England, though her feudal lord's lightest words were worth men's lives, and though the blood of the vexed husbandman dropped in the furrows of her fields than there is, while the animation of her multitudes is sent like fuel to feed the factory smoke, and the strength of them is given daily to be wasted into the fineness of a web or racked into the exactness of a llne."

"And what a slough (the slough of Despond in London) it is," says General Booth in his "Darkest England," "no man can gauge who has not waded therein, as some of us have done, up to the very neck for long years. Talk about Dante's Hell and all the horrors and cruelties of the torture-chamber of the lost ! The man who walks with open eyes and with bleeding heart through the shambles of our civilization needs no such fantastic images of the poet to teach him horror. Often and often when I have seen the young and the poor and the helpless go down before my eyes into the morass, trampled under foot by beasts of prey in human shape that haunt these regions, it seemed as if God were no longer in His world, but that in His stead reigned a fiend merciless as Hell, ruthless as the grave. Hard it is, no doubt, to read in Stanley's pages of the slave traders coldly arranging for the surprise of a village, the capture of the inhabitants, the massacre of those who resist, and the violation of all the women ; but the Stony Streets of London, if they could but speak, would tell of tragedies as awful, of ruin as complete, of ravishments as horrible, as if we were in Central Africa, only the ghastly devastation is covered, corpse-like, with the artificialities and hypocrisies of modern civilization."

Mr. G. Lowes Dickinson observes: "It is not really credible in the West, to be anything but a man of business in the widest sense of the term; to live in any way which cannot be shown directly or indirectly to increase the comforts and facilities of life or diminish its detriments......The pace at which we are living, the competition of every kind, the intensity, the fatigue, the nerve-strain, involve a dislocation of the moral equilibrium of life. The East lives, and has always lived at a lower tension; but it has kept a better balance between the active and contemplative faculties. It is in that balance that I see civilization."

Mr. E. B. Havell, a sincere well-wisher of India, advises the Indians: "None but the ignorant or charlatans will recommend you the paths of Western commercialism as leading to true national prosperity............Nowhere in India—not even in the direst time of famine and pestilence—is there such utter depravity, such helpless physical, moral and spiritual degradation as that which exists in the commercial cities of Europe directly brought about by modern industrial methods."

Max Nordau observes: "Mere sewage exhalations are played out. The filth of Zola's art and of his disciples in literary canal-dredging has been got over, and nothing remains for it but to turn to submerged peoples and social strata. The vanguard of civilization holds its nose at the pit of undiluted naturalism, and can only be brought to bend over it with sympathy and curiosity when by cunning engineering, a drain from the boudoir and sacristy has been turned into it. Mere sensuality passes as commonplace, and only finds admission when disguised as something unnatural and degenerate. Books treating of the relations between the sexes, with no matter how little reserve, seem too dully moral. Elegent titillation only begins when normal sexual relations leave off. Priapus has become a symbol of virtue. Vice looks to Sodom and Lesbos, to

Bluebeard's castle and the servants' hall of the 'divine' Marquis de Sade's *Justice* for its embodiments"

"From the great houses in the city of London to the village grocer," says Froude, "the commercial life of England has been saturated with fraud. So deep has it gone that a strictly honest tradesman can hardly hold his ground against competition. You can no longer trust that any article you buy is the thing which it pretnds to be. We have false weights, false measures, cheating and shoddy everywhere... .....We Londoners are poisoned in the water which we drink, poisoned in the gas with which we light our houses, we are poisoned in our bread, poisoned in our milk and butter, poisoned in the remedies for which, when these horrible compounds have produced their consequence, we in our simplicity apply to our druggist, while the druggists are in turn cheated by the swindling rogues that supply their medicines."

"The deterioration of our population in large towns," says General Booth "is one of the most undisputed facts of social economics. The country is the breeding ground of healthy citizens. But for the constant influx of countrydom, cockneydom would long ere this have perished. But unfortunately the country is being depopulated...........He (the country child) lives a natural life amid the birds and trees and growing crops and the animals of the fields. He is not a mere human ant crawling on the granite pavement of a great urban ants' nest, with an unnaturally developed nervous system and a sickly constitution."

"The sucking power of the towns", observes Sir Rider Haggard, "I consider to be the most serious and vital problem facing civilization to-day. The supposed advantages of the cities are drawing our people off the land, and changing them from solid, steady, dependable men and women to a race of neurotics who will ultimately be unable to cope with the stress of modern conditions.

We must at all costs, before it is too late, provide some means of preserving or recreating a class rooted in the land. The trend of people from the land to the cities has always preceded the downfall of nations, and there is no reason for supposing that Nature will alter her rule in this respect." "It looks," says Dean Inge, "as if Plato and Ruskin were right when they urged that the wealth that comes from trade is morally poisonous, and that we ought to go back to being a simple agricultural country. If these prophets are right, nothing will put an end to social discontent except the destruction of our great cities and great industries."

The revulsion of feeling against the modern industrial civilization is much more pronounced in India than in the West. It is in the fitness of things that it should be so. The Indian sages like the other seers of antiquity kept the development of industry within proper bounds. One of them, Manu, placed the establishment of huge machinery in the category of sins. Industrialisation and consequent urbanisation have not yet gone very far in India. The bulk of her population, some eighty per cent or so, still live in villages happy in their cultural Swaraj, however decadent it may be. What is urgently needed now is to protect them from the aggressive attacks of Western and Westernised, iconoclastic, revolutionary social and political roformers ; and it is to be hoped that the forces in favour of Indian culture will soon be sufficiently strong to do that. True, the mass of our people are superstitious.

But from the dawn of human history the multitude have always been more or less superstitious, have always been guided more or less by forms and formulas everywhere, even in societies which claim to be most highly civilized. It cannot be otherwise, and it will never be otherwise, unless there is a revolution in the mental constitution of man, of which there is no sign as yet. Life is so short, and the path of true knowledge is so long and so arduous, that real enlightenment must be the prerogative of the few. Compulsory education or no compulsory education, the 'man in the street,' is always more or less ignorant, and casts off one superstition only to take up another. If he ceases to believe in the efficacy of charms and relics, of pilgrimages and ablutions, of *Mantras* and *Yajnas* to secure his salvation, he forthwith begins to entertain a belief, no less superstitious (and much more injurious) in the efficacy of steam and electricity and of other scientific developments as a cure for the ills of life. He pulls down old gods and goddesses such as Siva, Vishnu, Christ, Virgin Mary and Kali, only to install new ones in their places, such as Wealth, War, Pleasure, Equality or Fatherland. If modern influences have shaken his belief in creation by the fiat of an Almighty Being, he has either ceased to believe in such a Being, or worse still, pays superstitious homage to a new deity denominated Evolution, and zealously propagates the cult of "Might is Right," of "Can I kill thee or canst thou kill me." If he casts off a superstitious belief in the gospel of Duty and Renunciation, he instantly begins to entertain a no less superstitious and much more harmful belief in the gospel of Right and Enjoyment.

The old superstitions did not do a fraction of the harm which the new ones are doing. Indeed, some of the former were distinctly beneficial to society. Such superstitious beliefs, for instance, as are entertained by the multitade, in the prowess of a Hanuman or Samson, in the devouring by a couple of she-bears of forty-two Jewish children for laughing at a prophet, in Jonah's whale harbouring "the disobedient prophet as an inside passenger," in the floating of the Noah's ark over a flooded world, or in the floating of an iron axe-head at the bidding of Elisha do no more harm to humanity than nursery tales or stories of Arabian Nights. On the other hand, superstitions like. idol-worship which is affected by people at a certain stage of mental evolution foster in the worshippers a frame of mind which is distinctly conducive to moral progress. There are ancient superstitions like the excessive reverence for the cow in India which are highly beneficial to society economically ; or those like the inclusion of drinking spirituous liquors in the category of sins which are of considerable hygienic importance. True, old superstitions like witchcraft and *Sati* resulted in barbarities. But, the atrocities attributable to them sink into utter insignificance compared to those ascribable to the wide propagation of the superstitious cult of survival of the fittest in "tooth and claw," and of the worship of Mammon and of Fatherland.

Mother India is usually regarded by her Western-educated sons, as an invalid ; and it is considered to be a point of patriotism with the great majority of them to try to restore her to health by the assiduous application of various foreign remedies. The fact that notwithstanding such application her condition has been deteriorating, instead of improving, during the last half century set me sometime ago to watch and observe her closely. The results of this observation are :—

First. That I have not noticed anything seriously wrong with her.

Secondly. That it is true, as I have just said , she has latterly been getting worse, and been exhibiting symptoms of an alarming character. This is, however, I firmly believe, mainly attributable to the injudicious application of unsuitable, exotic remedies.

But for these, Mother India would, I expect, be still as hale and hearty a dame as any might be expected to be at her age and the circumstances in which she is placed. She has, no doubt, long since passed the bloom, alertness and activity of her youth, but with them also the numerous snares and pitfalls to which youth is subject : and the best proof of her vitality and recuperative capacity is the fact, that she has sucessfully withstood the ravages of time for untold centuries. She does not make such a brave show as several of her proud and powerful young sisters of the West. Nevertheless, in all her native simplicity she appears to me to be radiant with an ethereal beauty, and a calm, healthy, beingnant expression which it would take the latter long to attain, if, indeed, they live long enough to attain it at all.

This is my humble answer to one of the charges which some of my¡Neo-Indian brethren who have the patience to go through this book will probably bring against me—the charge of pessimism. I am certainly pessimistic about the outlandish nostrums our Mother is plied with ; and the purpose of this work is to expose their injurious tendencies. But I am pessimistic about the remedies, because I am optimistic about the condition of the patient, because I am fully convinced that they are not suited to her constitution, and that they are aggravating rather than alleviating the insalutary effects of unavoidable causes of an adverse character, and are, on the whole, doing her more harm than good. Treated as an invalid, she is gradually becoming one, and losing confidence in her own recuperative power. She undoubtedly has her ailments. But, for them such drastic treatment in accordance with the methods and principles of an immature civilization as is resorted to by my Neo-Indian friends is quite uncalled for and is decidedly harmful.

From the conversations I have had with friends in regard to the views expressed in this work, I may anticipate another criticism of an adverse character—that I am destructive and have but little to offer by way of construction. On this point I have to observe :—

First. In reality, it is my Neo-Indian compatriots who have been destructive. Consciously or unconsciously, with the best of motives, no doubt, they have been doing their utmost to demolish an old structure with a safe and strong foundation which has hitherto afforded as happy a home as any nation may reasonably aspire to have, and to raise a new structure after the Western pattern. I have in this work endeavoured to show how very insecure the foundation of this new structure is, and how very illusory is the prospect of its affording a happier home than the one we are deserting. Thus, in one sense, the tendency of this work is destructive, but destructive of what I conceive to be an unsubstantial, though imposing "castle in the air" on the erection of which a good deal of energy is being wasted. In another sense, it is preservative, for in trying to pull down this newly started structure, I am indirectly seeking to preserve the old one.

Secondly. I confess I have nothing new to construct. Troughout this work I have shown my predilection for our modest old home. It certainly needs repairs, and 1 have given abundant hints as to the lines on which they should be done. While executing them we should be very careful not to impair its foundation. That foundation is culture, the essence of which is Vedantism. Benevolence has from remote antiquity been recognised as the basic principle of ethical culture. As long ago as B.C. 2435. the Chinese Emperor Kuh taught that no virtue is higher than to love all men. It is self-sacrificing benevolence that would bind the different classes and nations together, and direct the forces making for material progress to beneficent channels such as lead to the abiding welfare of mankind. And the propagation of genuine Indian culture would be a very effective way of promoting it in the East as well as in the West. Benevolence is of such supreme significance to humanity, that without it such present day movements and institutions as socialism and the League of Nations are either mischievous or useless, and with it, they are more or less superfluous. True, the fundamental principles of Indian culture are expounded every Sunday in Christian lands in thousands of sermons, and also in class lessons where education has not been entirely secularised. This is where the Indian view point of life and pedagogics differs from the Western. The life of the average present day Westerner is, if one may so express it, compartmental. He has one compartment reserved for religion and morality, and one for education and conduct. He generally locks up the former when he comes out of the church or the class for religion and morality. The Indian, on the other hand, views life as a whole in which religion, morality, education and conduct are all interblended. His ideal of education is to turn out a whole man, physically, intellectually, and above all, morally. The Western view has unquestionably led to extraordinary "efficiency," but to efficiency of a shortsighted character. It has led to material aggrandisement on a grand scale, but to an unstable, unhappy and discordant state of society, and, instead of mitigating the miseries of humanity, it has considerably added to them. The Indian view, on the other hand, has not resulted in material development at all comparable to what has been accomplished in the West, but has led to a much more stable and much happier state of society, and has not only done no harm to mankind, but has benefited it to no small extent. And we are strongly inclined to prefer the Indian to the Western view.

The Hindus are often characterised as unpractical dreamers given to excessive speculation. But using the term practical in a broad, long-sighted sense, I venture to think, the charge has no foundation in fact ; and their practicalness has been exhibited in nothing so much as in the way they sought to inculcate the basic principles of their pedagogics. They saw the comparative futility of sermons and class lessons in religion and morality. They are good in their way, but they do not go very far. There is no country in the world where Religion has been taught more extensively and more assiduously than in Germany. But, if the value of religious education is to be estimated by the extent to which it contributes to ethical development—and we do not know of any other rational way of estimating it—its comparative worthlessness is proved by the fact, that no country has exhibited greater moral perversity than Germany during the late Great War.

The Hindu sages instead of depending upon copy-book maxims and precepts ordered daily life so that the essential principles of culture might be ingrained in the constitution. The methods prescribed by them are Brahmacharya,* Bhuta-Yajna, Manushya-Yajna and Sandhya. No better methods have, to my knowledge, been discovered. They may be advantageously practised even by persons who do not profess any religion, whether free thinkers, agnostics or atheists. If the protagonists of Indian culture succeed in their efforts to revive it, they would do immense good not only to India but also to the entire civilized world.

* Brahmacharya inculcates a life of ascetic simplicity intended especially for students. Bhuta Yajna serves the purpose of cultivating humanitarian feeling towards all living beings. Manushya-Yajna, performed by the daily serving of a stranger irrespective of caste or creed, promotes universal benevolence. Sandhya is meditation accompanied by deep breathing twice or thrice a day.

BY THE SAME AUTHOR

I. EPOCHS OF CIVILIZATION

Cloth, pp. 339—xxii. Rs. 2.

"Valuable addition to historico-sociological literature. In his usual, simple, perspicuous and pleasant style, Mr. Bose enunciates in this book a theory of civilization which may not be altogether new, but which is laid down, for the first time, in a definite and categorical form and fully developed and elaborated by this learned and thoughtful writer."—*The Modern Review.*

"Mr. Bose puts his case with a sound judgment and a commendable restraint that make his book a valuable contribution to the study of history"—*The Literary Guide* (London).

"The author has his history most thoroughly at hand and his scientific training is evident not only in his illustrations but also the whole classification which he uses."—*The Calcutta Review.*

"In some of his conclusions and dicta, he (the author) even strikes a truer and more profound note than the Western writers on the subject............The Hindu's unerring sense of the spiritual has led to a valuable doctrine concerning the growth and stability of human civilization."—*The Indian Review.*

"Mr. Bose's book is a valuable one and deserves careful reading—*The Theosophist.*

"Mr. Bose is careful about his facts, his judgments are sensible and sober, and his style is simple, clear, and to the point........... His book deserves to be widely read."—*The Englishman.*

"Our only excuse (for the length of the review) is the importance of the subject and the fascination of the book..... ......It is a remarkable contribution to the science of Sociology"—*The Amrita Bazar Patrika.*

"A valuable contribution to the literature on the subject of the world's kulturgeschichte. The great merit of the book is its handy compass and the direct and philosophic way in which the complicated mass of details is marshalled."—*The Leader.*

"The author's distinguishing merit is the orderly arrangement and easy marshalling of the large quantity of material carefully selected and assimilated."—*The Bombay Chronicle.*

"This is a book of very great interest................ A book for all who think about things"—*The Indian Daily News.*

"The book is a very deep and close study of a very important problem, and in about 300 pages the author has given us a clear, well-reasoned and careful study of the chief civilizations of the world, their stages and developments, the factors which have built them up and the causes which make for their ultimate extinction."—*The Hindu Patriot.*

"In the narrow compass of a tiny volume, Mr. Bose has compressed some of the deepest and most accurate investigations into the history of civilization, and has marshalled his facts with a consummate mastery which leaves very little for the captious critic to cavil at."—*The Hindusthæn Review.*

II. SOME PRESENT-DAY SUPERSTITIONS.

CONTENTS: The Superstitions of Natural Science—The Superstition of Equality in the West—The Superstition of Equality in India—The Political Superstitions—The Drug Superstition—The "Education" Superstition—The "Progress" Superstition.

Cloth, pp. 260 Rs. 4

"While Mr. Bose appreciates the R. P. A and J. S. Mill and (very much) Herbert Spencer, and some other elements of European and American culture, he has resolved to expose, in fiery and ruthless language, such Western superstitions as the belief in Democracy, Socialism, Science (as an instrument of brotherhood), Equality, Drugs, Education, and Progress. If anything can shock us out of our "chaos" and "degeneration," this prophetic shout from Calcutta ought to do it. It is terrible, but it is worth reading."

The Literary Guide (London),

"The book is well worth reading as an excellent though perhaps too highly coloured picture of what Western Civilisation looks to an out-and-out admirer of India's past."—*The Pioneer.*

"We need books which tend to widen our vision, to extend our range of life, to correct old beliefs and to give wise data for our thinking. Mr. Pramatha Nath Bose's essay on "Some Present day Superstitions" must be regarded as such a book."

The Amrita Bazar Patrika

"Mr. Bose subjects each aspect of modern life to a merciless analysis..... .... With unerring judgment Mr. Bose has spotted the dangers and pitfalls to which civilization is liable to fall."—*United India and Indian States.*

"This book is a most interesting Study in the genesis and prevalence of erroneous hopes and beliefs.—*The Indian Review.*

"Mr. Bose is a thoughtful student and a prolific writer on subjects connected with ancient Hindu Civilization of which he is an ardent admirer. In this volume he cries down "modern" tendencies masquerading in the garb of Western imitation which he characterises as so many Superstitions."—*The Statesman.*

III. ESSAYS AND LECTURES

SECOND EDITION.

pp. 204 Rs. 2.

"The papers reprinted cover a wide range, and represent the thoughts and convictions of a quarter of a century. Mr. Bose has long been known as one of the most thoughtful Indians of our generation. His vast scientific knowledge is based on a wide outlook of human life, and the papers reprinted in the volume under notice ·· ....display in a remarkable degree wide and accurate knowledge of Indian problems—social and industrial. Mr. Bose's *Essays and Lectures*—which were buried in the files of journals and periodicals—fully deserve to be resuscitated and we are glad that they have been made available to the public. We recommend to educated Indians and Anglo-Indians a careful perusal of Mr. Bose's book, from a study of which one will certainly rise with a better and more accurate knowledge of some of the present-day problems of India."—*The Hindusthan Review.*

"This neatly printed book of over two hundred pages contains some of the speeches and magazine articles of Mr. P. N. Bose delivered and written between the years 1880–1917......... Few Indians can equal Mr. Bose in simplicity, gracefulness and felicity of style and we heartily commend this book to the public." *The Modern Review.*

"This collection...deals with many matters of vital importance to the welfare of Indian............... As this is a second edition we need not do more than call attention to the careful study which Mr. Bose has made of the grave situation caused by Western methods of production, and the able manner in which his recommendations are presented."—*New India,*

IV. SURVIVAL OF HINDU CIVILIZATION, PART II.

Physical Degeneration its causes and Remedies.

Cloth *pp.* 178 Rs. 1/8.

"We should very much like this book to be studied by all who are interested in the welfare of India and who do not desire that the Hindus would become extinct. It contains ample food for reflection.—*The Amrita Bazar Patrika.*

"He [Mr. Bose] develops this thesis and suggests a number of remedies which deserve careful consideration at the hands of his countrymen. A very thoughtful book."—*The Indian Daily News.*

"The book is not only exceedingly interesting, but deals with a problem of vital importance, and Mr. Bose's style and manner of presentation of his case are, as usual, charming. ....The book contains, however, material for serious reflection, and deserves wide circulation among those who think about the future of the country."—*The Modern Review.*

V. PAMPHLETS AT TWELVE ANNAS EACH

1. THE ROOT CAUSE OF THE GREAT WAR

"This little book is well worth study by those who are carried away by the glamour of western Civilization.' *The Modern Review.*

"A short but illuminative essay." *The Hindustan Review.*

"Mr. Bose gives a detached and independent view of the root causes of the war......His is a characteristically Hindu view." *The Indian Review.*

2. NATIONAL EDUCATION AND MODERN PROGRESS

"We have seldom come across a more thoughtful production He [the author] has exhaustively dealt with the problem of national education.'—*The Amrita Bazar Patrika.*

"Mr. P. N. Bose's book comes in good time. He advocates the introduction of national education with a passion born of a disgust for the Western system of learning which, as Lord Haldane says, subordinates education to examination.........On the whole it is an extremely interesting work that Mr. Bose has written. We heartily recommend the book to those who are interested in national education."—*The Bombay Chronicle.*

"Will be welcomed by all thoughtful men who care something for the education of their country's youth."—*The Hindu Message.*

"The subject matter is very thoughtful and suggestive and practical."—*The Mahamandal Magazine.*

3. THE ECONOMIC ASPECT OF THE MONTAGU CHELMSFORD REFORM SCHEME.

"Mr. Bose has pointed out the most vulnerable spot in the much vaunted Reform scheme," *Every man's Review.*

"Mr. Bose takes too pessimistic a view of the situation, but we must admit that the arguments by which he attempts to prove his point contain ample food for reflection."—*The Modern Review.*

4. GIVE THE PEOPLE BACK THEIR OWN (an open letter to his Excellency the Viceroy and Governor General of India.)

"We would very much like this book to be read by every one whose mind is working now at possible schemes for her political advancement." *Prabuddha Bharata.*

5. DEGENERATION—A WORLD PROBLEM.

"According to the author, and he quotes a number of well known European observers in support of his vew, the human race has of late degenerated both morally and physically. This degeneration he attributes to the materialistic civilization of the West in general and the industrial revolution in particular.. The book is interesting reading." *The Calcutta Review*

6. AN EASTERN VIEW OF WESTERN PROGRESS

(Reprinted from the *Westminister Review* and *East and West.*)

VI. PAMPHLETS AT SIX ANNAS EACH.

1. HINDU-MOSLEM AMITY.

"Of Great interest because of the wealth of historical illustration in which it abounds." *The Bombay Chronicle.*

2. THE MONTAGU-CHELMSFORD REFORM SCHEME AND INDIAN NATIONHOOD.

3. THE MONTAGU-CHEMSFORD REFORM SCHEME. A CONSTUCTIVE CRITICISM.